About This Resource

Why is this topic important?

The need for practical, relevant, and usable information about how to lead across differences is growing. The differences addressed in this Facilitator's Guide are steeped in social identities, such as those related to gender, religion, race, ethnicity, and country of origin. These are exceedingly difficult conversations to broach in a learning environment. This guide provides tools and advice to help you effectively plan and implement a session or course on leading across differences (LAD) based on the *Leading Across Differences Casebook*.

People learn from experience. By providing the experiences of others, such as the cases from the LAD casebook, and the information to help translate those experiences provided in this guide, participants will be better prepared for similar situations they may face or may better understand experiences they may have already had.

What can you achieve with this resource?

This Facilitator's Guide provides information to facilitators, trainers, and teachers on how to plan, select, and utilize cases and individual and group exercises in training sessions and courses to help leaders deal with difference. This guide also offers practical tips on effective facilitation and chapters of advice on how to deal with difficult conversations in the classroom, how to create safe and inclusive learning environments, using film to illustrate difference, and assessing and evaluating learning.

How is this resource organized?

The *Leading Across Differences* package consists of three components: the Casebook, this Facilitator's Guide, and an Instructor's Guide. The casebook presents the Leading Across Differences Framework, a series of case studies based on the Leading Across Differences research project, topical chapters by experts in the field, and a series of exercises. The material can be used for self-study or as part of a training or educational program. The *Leading Across Differences Facilitator's*

Guide provides detailed instructions for ways to utilize the cases and exercises and put together a training session to meet your audience's needs.

The Instructor's Guide provides syllabi and additional information unique to using the material in an educational setting. There are also five sets of PowerPoint presentations as part of the instructor's material. Instructors (college professors) are invited to download these free materials from the following site:

www.wiley.com/college/hannum

If you are a trainer (and not a college professor), please send an email to the following address to receive your free copy of these materials:

pfeiffertraining@wiley.com

Leading Across Differences:
Cases and Perspectives

Facilitator's Guide

Leading Across Differences: Cases and Perspectives

FACILITATOR'S GUIDE

Belinda B. McFeeters
Kelly M. Hannum
Lize Booysen

Pfeiffer
A Wiley Imprint
www.pfeiffer.com

Copyright © 2010 by John Wiley & Sons, Inc. All Rights Reserved.

Published by Pfeiffer
An Imprint of Wiley
989 Market Street, San Francisco, CA 94103-1741   www.pfeiffer.com

No part of this publication may be reproduced, stored in a retrieval system, or transmitted in any form or by any means, electronic, mechanical, photocopying, recording, scanning, or otherwise, except as permitted under Section 107 or 108 of the 1976 United States Copyright Act, without either the prior written permission of the Publisher, or authorization through payment of the appropriate per-copy fee to the Copyright Clearance Center, Inc., 222 Rosewood Drive, Danvers, MA 01923, 978-750-8400, fax 978-646-8600, or on the web at www.copyright.com. Requests to the Publisher for permission should be addressed to the Permissions Department, John Wiley & Sons, Inc., 111 River Street, Hoboken, NJ 07030, 201-748-6011, fax 201-748-6008, or online at http://www.wiley.com/go/permissions.

Limit of Liability/Disclaimer of Warranty: While the publisher and author have used their best efforts in preparing this book, they make no representations or warranties with respect to the accuracy or completeness of the contents of this book and specifically disclaim any implied warranties of merchantability or fitness for a particular purpose. No warranty may be created or extended by sales representatives or written sales materials. The advice and strategies contained herein may not be suitable for your situation. You should consult with a professional where appropriate. Neither the publisher nor author shall be liable for any loss of profit or any other commercial damages, including but not limited to special, incidental, consequential, or other damages.

Readers should be aware that Internet websites offered as citations and/or sources for further information may have changed or disappeared between the time this was written and when it is read.

For additional copies/bulk purchases of this book in the U.S. please contact 800-274-4434.

Pfeiffer books and products are available through most bookstores. To contact Pfeiffer directly call our Customer Care Department within the U.S. at 800-274-4434, outside the U.S. at 317-572-3985, fax 317-572-4002, or visit www.pfeiffer.com.

Pfeiffer also publishes its books in a variety of electronic formats. Some content that appears in print may not be available in electronic books.

Facilitator's Guide SKU #: 978KPART10865

Facilitator's Guide Package ISBN: 9780470566893

Facilitator's Guide Set ISBN: 9780470563359

Acquiring Editors:	Lisa Shannon
Assistant Editor:	Marisa Kelley
Marketing Manager:	Tolu Babalola
Director of Development:	Kathleen Dolan Davies
Developmental Editor:	Susan Rachmeler
Production Editor:	Michael Kay
Editor:	Rebecca Taff
Manufacturing Supervisor:	Becky Morgan

Printed in the United States of America

Printing   10 9 8 7 6 5 4 3 2

About Pfeiffer

Pfeiffer serves the professional development and hands-on resource needs of training and human resource practitioners and gives them products to do their jobs better. We deliver proven ideas and solutions from experts in HR development and HR management, and we offer effective and customizable tools to improve workplace performance. From novice to seasoned professional, Pfeiffer is the source you can trust to make yourself and your organization more successful.

Essential Knowledge Pfeiffer produces insightful, practical, and comprehensive materials on topics that matter the most to training and HR professionals. Our Essential Knowledge resources translate the expertise of seasoned professionals into practical, how-to guidance on critical workplace issues and problems. These resources are supported by case studies, worksheets, and job aids and are frequently supplemented with CD-ROMs, websites, and other means of making the content easier to read, understand, and use.

Essential Tools Pfeiffer's Essential Tools resources save time and expense by offering proven, ready-to-use materials—including exercises, activities, games, instruments, and assessments—for use during a training or team-learning event. These resources are frequently offered in looseleaf or CD-ROM format to facilitate copying and customization of the material.

Pfeiffer also recognizes the remarkable power of new technologies in expanding the reach and effectiveness of training. While e-hype has often created whizbang solutions in search of a problem, we are dedicated to bringing convenience and enhancements to proven training solutions. All our e-tools comply with rigorous functionality standards. The most appropriate technology wrapped around essential content yields the perfect solution for today's on-the-go trainers and human resource professionals.

Pfeiffer
www.pfeiffer.com
Essential resources for training and HR professionals

ABOUT THE CENTER FOR CREATIVE LEADERSHIP

The Center for Creative Leadership (CCL) is a top-ranked, global provider of executive education that develops better leaders through its exclusive focus on leadership education and research. Founded in 1970 as a nonprofit, educational institution, CCL helps clients worldwide cultivate creative leadership—the capacity to achieve more than imagined by thinking and acting beyond boundaries—through an array of programs, products, and other services.

Ranked in the top ten in the *Financial Times* annual executive education survey, CCL is headquartered in Greensboro, North Carolina, with campuses in Colorado Springs, Colorado; San Diego, California; Brussels, Belgium; and Singapore. Supported by more than five hundred faculty members and staff, it works annually with more than twenty thousand leaders and three thousand organizations. In addition, sixteen Network Associates around the world offer selected CCL programs and assessments.

CCL draws strength from its nonprofit status and educational mission, which provide unusual flexibility in a world where quarterly profits often drive thinking and direction. It has the freedom to be objective, wary of short-term trends, and motivated foremost by its mission—hence our substantial and sustained investment in leadership research. Although CCL's work is always grounded in a strong foundation of research, it focuses on achieving a beneficial impact in the real world. Its efforts are geared to be practical and action oriented, helping leaders and their organizations more effectively achieve their goals and vision. The desire to transform learning and ideas into action provides the impetus for CCL's programs, assessments, publications, and services.

CAPABILITIES

CCL's activities encompass leadership education, knowledge generation and dissemination, and building a community centered on leadership. CCL is broadly recognized for excellence in executive education, leadership development, and innovation by sources such as *BusinessWeek, Financial Times, The New York Times,* and The *Wall Street Journal.*

OPEN-ENROLLMENT PROGRAMS

Fourteen open-enrollment courses are designed for leaders at all levels, as well as people responsible for leadership development and training at their organizations. This portfolio offers distinct choices for participants seeking a particular learning environment or type of experience. Some programs are structured specifically around small group activities, discussion, and personal reflection, while others offer hands-on opportunities through business simulations, artistic exploration, team-building exercises, and new-skills practice. Many of these programs offer private one-on-one sessions with a feedback coach.

For a complete listing of programs, visit http://www.ccl.org/programs.

CUSTOMIZED PROGRAMS

CCL develops tailored educational solutions for more than one hundred client organizations around the world each year. Through this applied practice, CCL structures and delivers programs focused on specific leadership development needs within the context of defined organizational challenges, including innovation, the merging of cultures, and the development of a broader pool of leaders. The objective is to help organizations develop, within their own cultures, the leadership capacity they need to address challenges as they emerge.

Program details are available online at http://www.ccl.org/custom.

COACHING

CCL's suite of coaching services is designed to help leaders maintain a sustained focus and generate increased momentum toward achieving their goals. These coaching alternatives vary in depth and duration and serve a variety of needs, from helping an executive sort through career and life issues to working with an organization to integrate coaching into its internal development process. Our coaching offerings, which can supplement program attendance or be customized for specific individual or team needs, are based on our ACS model of assessment, challenge, and support.

Learn more about CCL's coaching services at http://www.ccl.org/coaching.

ASSESSMENT AND DEVELOPMENT RESOURCES

CCL pioneered 360-degree feedback and believes that assessment provides a solid foundation for learning, growth, and transformation and that development truly happens when an individual recognizes the need to change. CCL offers a broad selection of assessment tools, online resources, and simulations that can help individuals, teams, and organizations increase their self-awareness, facilitate their own learning, enable their development, and enhance their effectiveness.

CCL's assessments are profiled at http://www.ccl.org/assessments.

PUBLICATIONS

The theoretical foundation for many of our programs, as well as the results of CCL's extensive and often groundbreaking research, can be found in the scores of publications issued by CCL Press and through the center's alliance with Jossey-Bass, a Wiley imprint. Among these are landmark works, such as *Breaking the Glass Ceiling* and *The Lessons of Experience,* as well as quick-read guidebooks focused on core aspects of leadership. CCL publications provide insights and practical advice to help individuals become more effective leaders, develop leadership training within organizations, address issues of change and diversity, and build the systems and strategies that advance leadership collectively at the institutional level.

A complete listing of CCL publications is available at http://www.ccl.org/publications.

LEADERSHIP COMMUNITY

To ensure that the Center's work remains focused, relevant, and important to the individuals and organizations it serves, CCL maintains a host of networks, councils, and learning and virtual communities that bring together alumni, donors, faculty, practicing leaders, and thought leaders from around the globe. CCL also forges relationships and alliances with individuals, organizations, and associations that share its values and mission. The energy, insights, and support from these relationships help shape and sustain CCL's educational and research practices and provide its clients with an added measure of motivation and inspiration as they continue their lifelong commitment to leadership and learning.

To learn more, visit http://www.ccl.org/community.

RESEARCH

CCL's portfolio of programs, products, and services is built on a solid foundation of behavioral science research. The role of research at CCL is to advance the understanding of leadership and to transform learning into practical tools for participants and clients. CCL's research is the hub of a cycle that transforms knowledge into applications and applications into knowledge, thereby illuminating the way organizations think about and enact leadership and leader development.

Find out more about current research initiatives at http://www.ccl.org/research.

For additional information about CCL, please visit http://www.ccl.org or call Client Services at (336) 545-2810.

CONTENTS

Introduction	1
PART ONE Planning and Running a Session	3
The Advice Chapters	3
Exercises	4
Learning Outcomes	7
Overview of Case Format	10
Selecting a Case	11
Assigning Additional Reading	11
Creating a Session Agenda	13
Facilitation Tips	17
PART TWO Advice Chapters	21
Chapter 1: Handling Difficult Conversations in the Classroom by Terrell L. Strayhorn	27
Chapter 2: Teaching Inclusion by Example and Experience: Creating an Inclusive Learning Environment by Bernardo M. Ferdman	37
Chapter 3: Building Safe Learning Environments by Laurien Alexandre	51
Chapter 4: Using Film to Illustrate Different Perspectives by Clemson Turregano and Belinda B. McFeeters	63
Chapter 5: Assessing Leadership Across Differences Sessions by Emily Hoole	73

PART THREE	Individual Exercises	83
Exercise 1:	Mapping Your Social Identities	85
Exercise 2:	Your Experience with Triggers	95
Exercise 3:	Identifying Faultlines	101
Exercise 4:	Cultural Values	105
Exercise 5:	Approaches to Difference	109
Exercise 6:	Cultural Intelligence (CQ)	115
Exercise 7:	Your Leadership Practices	119
Exercise 8:	Examining Your Leadership Networks	125
Exercise 9:	Taking a New Perspective	131
PART FOUR	Group and Paired Exercises	137
Exercise 1:	Seeking Another Perspective on Social Identity	139
Exercise 2:	Your Experience with Triggers	143
Exercise 3:	Identifying Faultlines	145
Exercise 4:	Cultural Values	147
Exercise 5:	Approaches to Difference	149
Exercise 6:	Cultural Intelligence (CQ)	153
Exercise 7:	Your Leadership Practices	159
Exercise 8:	Examining Leadership Networks	161
Exercise 9:	Exploring Mental Models of Leadership	165
Exercise 10:	Using Film in the Classroom to Illustrate Difference	167
Resources		169
References		179
About the Contributors		185
About the Editors		187

Introduction

Leading across difference, diversity management, multiculturalism, inclusion, tolerance, and inclusive leadership are all hot topics and important concepts in today's workplaces. If we value diversity, are inclusive, and lead effectively across difference, we can be more productive. If we don't do these things, conflict and negative emotion will surely follow.

We stated in the introduction to the casebook that, despite the growing challenges and opportunities created by our interconnected world, many people do not know how to lead through situations in which there are misunderstandings or conflicts rooted in differences. Yet, very little time is spent preparing leaders to understand their roles and to take appropriate action, mainly because few practical resources exist that offer solutions that are grounded in research. An important tenet in working effectively across difference is to treat people as individuals, with multiple identities, while also having an appreciation of their membership in particular groups. The key is to focus on both differences and similarities that can be capitalized on—to realize that no one, no single group, has all the answers, but that together we can accomplish great things.

This Facilitator's Guide provides information to facilitators on how to select and utilize cases, individual exercises, and group exercises in training sessions and courses.

PURPOSE

This guide is a supplement to the *Leading Across Differences* casebook. In this guide, we provide facilitators with guidance and advice for using the casebook in a variety of learning environments. We focus on using the casebook in group settings, whether the meetings occur online or face-to-face, and providing facilitators with additional tools and ideas to creatively and effectively use the cases. While the casebook is written so learners can read and reflect on the material as part of a self-study program, to reap full benefit of the cases it is helpful to engage with others in discussions of the ideas and events; facilitating those discussions is the focus of this guide.

AUDIENCE

The primary audience for this guide is facilitators, of any sort, using the *Leading Across Differences* casebook in group settings. The guide is appropriate for facilitators working in corporations, government agencies, nonprofit organizations, and universities. The casebook itself can be used by new or budding managers, supervisors, or leaders who will be (or are) leading and working in groups with varied social identity groups represented.

ABOUT THIS GUIDE

The Facilitator's Guide is divided into four parts: (1) planning and running of a session, (2) advice chapters, (3) individual exercises, and (4) group exercises. Resources and a reference list are included at the end of this guide. Accompanying materials include the casebook, *Leading Across Differences: Cases and Perspectives,* which offers thirteen cases based on real incidents in organizations in conjunction with analytical tools for addressing the dynamics of difference in organizations, and an Instructor's Guide, which is available online and provides additional information specific to using the casebook and the Facilitator's Guide in an academic setting.

PART ONE

Planning and Running a Session

This portion of the Facilitator's Guide provides information on the learning objectives and logistics of the sessions, the case descriptions, and how to select and utilize the cases. It also provides general facilitation tips and guidelines on creating a course agenda and assigning additional reading and group exercises, either in preparation for or reflection after the training.

THE ADVICE CHAPTERS

The advice chapters (Part II) in the Facilitator's Guide have been written by experts who share their insights and experiences about how to facilitate training sessions about learning to effectively work across differences. Effective leadership across difference rests on deep self-awareness as well as an awareness of other perspectives. Striking a balance between those two dynamics can be difficult; the advice chapters can help prepare you, as a facilitator, to create and maintain that balance.

The first three chapters in this part of the Facilitator's Guide provide a foundational understanding of the most important core skills needed to facilitate training sessions to lead effectively across difference. Dr. Terrell Strayhorn provides an overview of handling difficult conversations in the classroom; he presents examples and practical guidelines. Dr. Bernardo Ferdman discusses how to create an inclusive learning environment through illustrating how to teach inclusion by example and experience. Dr Laurien Alexandre describes by way of examples how to build safe learning environments to teach in and for personal growth and development.

The last two chapters in this section deal with specific aspects of facilitated training. Drs. Clemson Turregano and Belinda McFeeters provide guidelines on how to use film to illustrate different perspectives in training sessions. The last advice chapter, by Dr. Emily Hoole, describes the theory and practice of assessing learning and development in training.

EXERCISES

Individual Exercises (Part III)

The individual exercises are designed for either self-study or for use in a training or classroom setting. The learning objectives, materials needed, and instructions are provided for each exercise. In general, the exercises prompt deeper reflection about oneself, others, and the context in which the relationship is embedded. As a facilitator, it is a good idea to complete the exercises prior to assigning them to participants, to gain a general understanding of the intended outcomes, and so that you will be aware of potential questions and responses. All of the individual exercises are included in the casebook, though some of the wording has been altered.

Group Exercises (Part IV)

The group and paired exercises are designed for use in a training or classroom setting with medium to large groups. Some of the group exercises can be used in conjunction with the individual exercises and are noted as such. The learning objectives, materials needed, links to relevant cases and chapters, as well as general instructions, are provided for each exercise. As with the individual exercises, the group and paired exercises also prompt deeper reflection about oneself, others, and the context in relation to dealing with difference.

Using Exercises

You are likely to be working with one of three general types of groups:

1. Groups in which people do not know each other,
2. Groups in which people know each other, but there is tension between them, or

3. Groups in which participants know and like/trust each other, at least to some extent.

Group and paired exercises in this guide have generally been written for those in the third group; however, as necessary, we have also included ideas for modifying the exercises for participants who fall in the other two types of groups.

It is important for you, as the facilitator, to create an environment that encourages, but does not force, everyone's active participation. When working with groups, stress the importance of having openness and mutual respect for one another. Explain that working with someone new allows for a fresh perspective, which is often a valuable asset for effective leaders.

Warm-Up Exercises

Various trust-building exercises are particularly helpful to use at the beginning of sessions with individuals who have tenuous relationships or those who do not know one another well. For example, guided activities in which one person verbally guides his or her blindfolded partner through some type of maze to accomplish a specific team goal serve as an opportunity to build trust among strangers or those with strained relationships.

Team-building exercises can also enhance group interactions. The "human knot," for example, is a fun exercise that requires participants, without speaking, to link hands with one another to form a human knot and then to strategically untie their knot. See http://leadership.uoregon.edu/resources/exercises_tips/team_builders/human_knot for specific details.

After team-building exercises, participants tend to feel more comfortable, relaxed, and more trusting of others in the room. After each exercise, it is important to use debriefing questions that emphasize participants' ability to work with one another to meet a goal or solve a problem. Once you have determined that some level of trust or confidence has been established among participants who have had tenuous relationships in the past or who do not know each other well, it becomes a bit of an easier task in regard to participating in the group and paired exercises included in this Facilitator's Guide.

Exercises in This Guide

Remind participants of the session purpose and re-emphasize the value of embracing difference, understanding diverse others, and making a commitment to becoming more effective at leading through conflict and across differences. For more detailed information, refer to the advice chapters in this guide and particularly the "Handling Difficult Conversations in the Classroom," the "Teaching Inclusion by Example and Experience: Creating an Inclusive Learning Environment," and the "Building Safe Learning Environments" chapters for techniques and tips for working with specific types of groups.

The list below outlines which exercises are particularly relevant to each case.

Individual Exercises	Cases
1. Mapping Your Social Identities	1 through 13
2. Your Experience with Triggers	1 through 13
3. Identifying Faultlines	5, 6, 8, 9, 10, 11, 12, 13
4. Cultural Values	2 through 13
5. Approaches to Difference	6, 9, 11, 13
6. Cultural Intelligence (CQ)	1, 2, 3, 4, 5, 12
7. Your Leadership Practices	1, 3, 4, 5, 6, 9, 10, 11, 12, 13
8. Examining Your Leadership Networks	2, 5, 6, 7, 11, 13
9. Taking a New Perspective	1 through 13

Group and Paired Exercises	Cases
1. Seeking Another Perspective on Social Identity	1 through 13
2. Your Experience with Triggers	1 through 13
3. Identifying Faultines	5, 6, 8, 9, 10, 11, 12, 13
4. Cultural Values	2 through 13
5. Approaches to Difference	6, 9, 11, 13
6. Cultural Intelligence (CQ)	1, 2, 3, 4, 5, 12
7. Your Leadership Practices	1, 3, 4, 5, 6, 9, 10, 11, 12, 13
8. Examining Leadership Networks	2, 5, 6, 7, 11, 13
9. Exploring Mental Models of Leadership	1, 3, 4, 8, 10, 13
10. Using Film in the Classroom to Illustrate Difference	No specific cases (Facilitators should design their own purposeful viewing questions relative to each film viewed.)

LEARNING OUTCOMES

Various learning outcomes can be addressed through the use of the individual and group/paired exercises. Tables 1 and 2 list the learning outcomes for each exercise so that you may determine which exercises are most appropriate to help your participants reach their goals.

Table 1
Individual Exercises and Learning Outcomes

Exercise	Learning Outcomes
1. *Mapping Your Social Identities* (page 85)	• Articulate one's given identity, chosen identity, and core identity. • Identify the influence social identity has on others and the leadership implications.
2. *Your Experience with Triggers* (page 95)	• Identify and understand how one's experiences with triggering events align with social and power conflicts in society at large. • List solutions that an individual or an organization can implement to prevent faultline activation and conflict in the future.
3. *Identifying Faultlines* (page 101)	• Identify potential faultlines in groups or teams.
4. *Cultural Values* (page 105)	• Articulate the role one's preferred cultural values play in decision, making and how values impact others. • Recognize how cultural value orientations impact decision making.
5. *Approaches to Difference* (p. 109)	• Define xenophobia and allophilia. • Identify one's orientation to social identity differences. • Develop ways to improve future encounters with individuals from different social identity groups.
6. *Cultural Intelligence* (page 115)	• Define cultural intelligence and the following factors: motivational CQ, cognitive CQ, meta-cognitive CQ, and behavioral CQ. • Describe how cultural intelligence factors impact leadership effectiveness in different settings.

(continued overleaf)

Table 1
(*continued*)

Exercise	Learning Outcomes
7. *Your Leadership Practices* (page 119)	• Identify leadership practice preferences for managing social identity conflict. • Articulate and apply the steps in the Leadership Response Cycle.
8. *Examining Your Leadership Networks* (page 125)	• Describe the benefits of networking with others from different social identity groups. • Identify strategies to enhance one's networks and become more effective at leadership networking.
9. *Taking a New Perspective* (page 131)	• Appreciate another social identity group's perspectives and experiences.

Table 2
Group/Paired Exercises and Learning Outcomes

Exercise	Learning Outcomes
1. *Seeking Another Perspective on Social Identity* (page 139)	• Understand different perspectives on one's social identity. • Challenge assumptions about others' social identities. • Describe how social identity can help or hinder the ability to make connections with others.
2. *Your Experience with Triggers* (page 143)	• Articulate the role values play in responding to triggering events. • Identify alternative ways to respond to triggering.

Table 2
(*continued*)

Exercise	Learning Outcomes
3. *Identifying Faultlines* (page 145)	• Explain faultline dynamics in groups or teams. • Identify potential faultlines in groups or teams.
4. *Cultural Values* (page 147)	• Articulate the role one's preferred cultural values play in decision making, and how values impact others. • Recognize how cultural value orientations impact decision making.
5. *Approaches to Difference* (page 149)	• Define xenophobia and allophilia. • Identify one's orientation to social identity differences. • Develop ways to improve future encounters with individuals from different social identity groups.
6. *Cultural Intelligence* (CQ) (page 153)	• Define cultural intelligence and the following factors: motivational CQ, cognitive CQ, metacognitive CQ, and behavioral CQ. • Describe how cultural intelligence factors impact leadership effectiveness in different settings. • Create a plan to enhance one's CQ.
7. *Your Leadership Practices* (page 159)	• Identify leadership practice preferences for managing social identity conflict. • Articulate the strengths and weaknesses of various leadership practices.
8. *Examining Leadership Networks* (page 161)	• Describe the collective benefits of networking with different social identity groups. • Identify strategies to enhance a group's networks and to become more effective at leadership networking.

(*continued overleaf*)

Table 2
(continued)

Exercise	Learning Outcomes
9. *Exploring Mental Models of Leadership* (page 165)	• Identify different perspectives on effective leadership. • Articulate the influence social identity has on one's mental model of leadership. • Describe how mental models of leadership influence expectations of leaders.
10. *Using Film in the Classroom to Illustrate Difference* (page 167)	*Note:* This approach can be used to meet a variety of learning outcomes. Facilitators must identify a learning outcome appropriate to their session and then apply this approach with that outcome (or outcomes) in mind.

OVERVIEW OF CASE FORMAT

The cases, which are included in the casebook, are short enough to be read and discussed in a session of an hour or more. You may choose to focus on only one aspect of a case if time is limited. Or you may choose to use the cases as a starting point for a much longer discussion of broad concepts and issues that takes place over multiple sessions. We have created the cases and supporting instructional materials to be flexible enough to meet multiple learning needs and formats. All of the cases follow the same format. Each case includes the following elements:

- A title,
- The type of trigger,
- The type of organization,
- Recommended chapters (from the casebook),
- A detailed description of the context and the event, and
- Discussion questions.

The discussion questions provided with each case are there for reference and to prompt your thinking—there are no right answers. You may choose to create your own discussion questions based on the learning objectives of your session. It is not essential to discuss all of the questions, and not all of the questions may be relevant to the key concepts and points you want to address. You may also want to use discussion questions as prompts for private or shared reflections of participants. For instance, students could write private journal entries or post their comments on shared blogs.

SELECTING A CASE

The case matrix shown in Table 3 is designed to provide details specific to each of the cases discussed in this book. Cases are organized by case number. For each case the following information is provided: country in which the case takes place, type of organization (FP = for-profit or NP = nonprofit), type of trigger (for a brief description, see Part 1 of the casebook; for more detail, see the chapter on triggers in Part 3 of the casebook), and the social identities (gender, race, religion, nationality, class, sexuality, language, immigrant status, education, and age) that are most closely related to the case. Social identities most relevant to the case are noted with dark gray shading, while those with secondary relevance to the case are noted with light gray shading. In some instances, more than one social identity was found to have the same or similar relevance to the case study. In these cases, multiple identities are noted with the appropriate shading. Social identities that are not directly relevant to the cases are not shaded.

ASSIGNING ADDITIONAL READING

The first four chapters in Part 3 of the casebook provide a foundational understanding of the core concepts running throughout the cases. Subsequent chapters go more deeply into the concepts illustrated in the cases. We highly recommend that facilitators read all of the foundational chapters in the casebook and provide a detailed overview of the concepts for participants. While all of the remaining chapters are relevant to the cases, we have listed on the next page places where there are connections between chapters and cases.

Table 3
Case Description Matrix

Case Number	Country	Org. Type	Trigger	Gender	Race	Religion	Nationality	Class	Sexuality	Language	Immigrant Status	Education	Age
1	South Africa	NP	Differential Treatment	■									■
2	Singapore	FP	Insult/ Humiliating Act				■				■		
3	United States	NP	Differential Treatment			■			■				
4	Hong Kong	FP	Assimilation			■	■						
5	Hong Kong	FP	Different Values										
6	United States	FP	Assimilation		■		■			■			
7	South Africa	FP	Assimilation		■					■			
8	South Africa	FP	Differential Treatment	■									
9	Jordan	FP	Differential Treatment				■				■		
10	Brazil	FP	Assimilation	■		■							
11	Jordan	NP	Simple Contact										
12	United States	NP	Differential Treatment						■				
13	France	FP	Differential Treatment					■				■	

Cases Most Relevant to Each Chapter

Chapter	Cases
1. Social Identity	1 through 13
2. Triggers of Social Identity Conflict	1 through 13
3. Organizational Faultlines	1 through 13
4. Leadership Practices Across Social Identity Groups	1through 13
5. Cultural Values	1, through 13
6. Approaches to Difference: Allophilia and Xenophobia	3, 5, 6, 9, 11, 12, 13
7. Cultural Intelligence	1, 2, 3, 4, 5, 6,12
8. Social Justice and Dignity	1 through 13
9. Miasma	1, 2, 3,5, 6, 7, 8, 9, 10, 11, 12, 13
10. Leading Across Cultural Groups	1 through 13
11. Leader Values and Authenticity	1 through 13
12. Leading Through Paradox	1 through 13

In addition, if you choose to assign supplemental readings, keep these general tips in mind:

1. Relevance to the subject matter. Choose meaningful readings that are closely related and expound on an important aspect of the subject matter.

2. Learning outcomes. Ensure that supplemental readings will contribute to the expected learning outcomes.

3. Time. Consider the time available for participants to read. Choose short, supplemental readings, as appropriate, to ensure participants have adequate time to complete each reading in its entirety.

CREATING A SESSION AGENDA

This section provides ideas about creating a session agenda to help participants reach a specific goal. Though each of the resources in the casebook and Facilitator's Guide are in some way relevant to one another, the three examples below are our suggestions for the *most* relevant components you can use to address the topics noted. You may choose to use our suggested agendas or pull ideas from this list to create your own.

The section begins with general directions for three different length sessions, then provides specific materials for sessions on understanding social identity, triggers, and leadership practices.

Full-Day Session

1. Assign casebook chapter readings prior to the session or allow time during the session to review.
2. Assign other readings from the Resources list or elsewhere.
3. Show one full-length film or a film clip if time permits.
4. Choose three or four of the recommended cases for group discussion.
5. Facilitate the suggested group exercise.

Half-Day Session

1. Follow the same agenda as the full-day session except show only the portions of your film choice that focus on your intended outcomes.
2. Limit the casebook chapter readings so as not to overwhelm participants.
3. Choose one of the recommended cases to review and discuss as a group.
4. Facilitate the group exercise if time permits.

One- to Two-Hour Session

1. Prepare a brief overview of the casebook chapter readings.
2. Have participants complete the group exercise.
3. Choose one of the recommended cases to review and discuss as a group.

I. Understanding Social Identity

Objective: Understand various aspects of one's social identity, the influence social identity has on others, and the different leadership implications that exist.

Introductory Materials

- Chapter 1: Social Identity: Understanding the In-Group/Out-Group Group Phenomenon
- Chapter 4: Leadership Practices Across Social Identity Groups
- Facilitator's Guide Chapters: Aspects of each chapter can assist with your agenda in some way.

Suggested Cases: 1 through 13
Group Exercise: 1

Additional Resources

Books:

- Haslam, S.A., van Knippenberg, D., Platow, M.J., & Ellemers N. (Eds.). (2003). *Social identity at work: Developing theory for organizational practice.* Philadelphia: Psychology Press.
- Plummer, D.L. (2003). *Handbook of diversity management: Beyond awareness to competency-based learning.* Lanham, MD: University Press of America.

Article:

- Nkomo, S.M., & Stewart M. (2006). Diverse identities in organizations. In S. Clegg, C. Hardy, & W. Nord (Eds.), *The Sage handbook of organisational studies* (2nd ed.). London: Sage.

Films:

- Ross, G. (1998). *Pleasantville.* Incorporates themes around diversity, individual change, cultural change, societal change, and community change. *Pleasantville* uses color to show diversity, change, loss of identity, and a resistance to change. Running time: 2 hours 3 minutes. Rated: PG-13
- Singleton, J. (1995). *Higher Learning.* People from various walks of life are faced with racial tension, responsibility, rape, and the meaning of getting a college education on a majority campus. Running time: 2 hours 7 minutes Rated: R

II. Triggers

Objective: To better understand triggering events and generate alternative solutions for responding to them.

Introductory Materials

- Casebook Chapter: Chapter 2: Triggers of Social Identity Conflict
- Facilitator's Guide Chapters: Aspects of each chapter can assist with your agenda in some way.

Suggested Cases: 1 through 13
Group Exercise: 2

Additional Resources

Books:

- Kossek, E.E., Lobel, S.A., & Brown, J. (2005). Human resource strategies to manage workforce diversity. In A. Konrad, P. Prasad, & J. K. Pringle (Eds.), *Handbook of workplace diversity* (pp. 53–74). London: Sage.

- Plummer, D.L. (2003). *Handbook of diversity management: Beyond awareness to competency-based learning.* Lanham, MD: University Press of America.

Articles:

- Chrobot-Mason, D., Ruderman, M.N., Weber, T.J., Ohlott, P.J., & Dalton, M.A. (2007). Illuminating a cross-cultural leadership challenge: When identity groups collide. *The International Journal of Human Resource Management*, *18*(11), 2011–2036.

- Homan, A.C., & Jehn, K.A. (2010). How leaders can make diverse groups less difficult: The role of attitudes and perceptions of diversity. In S. Schuman (Ed.), *The handbook for working with difficult groups: How they are difficult, why they are difficult, and what you can do.* San Francisco: Jossey-Bass.

Films:

- Haggis, P. (2004). *Crash*. Several stories interweave during two days in Los Angeles involving several diverse characters from all walks of life dealing with various incidents around race, class, and justice. Running time: 112 minutes. Rated: R

- Mun Wah, L. (1995). *The Color of Fear*. Oakland, CA. Racially diverse group spend a weekend together and dialogue about institutional and individual racism. Running time: 90 minutes. No rating noted.

III. Leadership Practices

Objective: To shed light on diverse preferences and leadership practices for managing social identity conflict.

Introductory Materials

- Chapter 4: Leadership Practices Across Social Identity Groups
- Facilitator's Guide Chapter: Aspects of each chapter can assist with your agenda in some way.

Suggested Cases: 1, 3, 4, 5, 6, 9, 10, 11, 12, 13
Group Exercise: 7

Additional Resources

Book:

- Linsky, M., & Heifetz, R. (2002). *Leadership on the line: Staying alive through the dangers of leading.* Boston: Harvard Business School Press.

Article:

- Chrobot-Mason, D., Ruderman, M.N., Weber, T.J., Ohlott, P.J., & Dalton, M. (2007). Illuminating a cross-cultural leadership challenge: When identity groups collide. *The International Journal of Human Resource Management, 18(11)*, 2011–2036.

FACILITATION TIPS

While this book does not focus on helping you develop all the competencies needed to facilitate leader and leadership development sessions, it does explicate the skills particularly important to be successful in facilitating effective leading across difference training sessions. For example, you, as the facilitator, should possess or seek training to enhance various competencies such as *self-knowledge or self-awareness* and understand how your personal beliefs may affect others and influence your facilitation style. You should emphasize the value of *embracing and managing difference* and have the ability to relay these values to individuals in the workplace or classroom. In addition, *preparation, maintaining control of the class, delivery, active listening, questioning, and mindful and respectful inquiry* are facilitation skills that should be utilized to ensure that the exchange of ideas and understandings is done in the most effective manner and to facilitate leading across difference training sessions. The advice chapters in this Facilitator's

Guide also discuss a number of valuable facilitation strategies, which include the following:

General Facilitation Tips

- Listen carefully and be respectful of all participants.
- Hold all participants in positive regard and value their contributions.
- Do not make quick judgments; listen.
- Prevent dominant consensus from silencing minority dissent (regardless of your own convictions); give voice to all.
- Use dialogue strategies to provide space for voice, silence, and listening.
- Model how to have discussions about " isms" without making it personal.
- Intervene without pushing the offender in a corner when offensive things are being said.
- Don't pretend to know everything; allow for self-vulnerability.
- Support ways of learning together by common readings, shared experiences, and learner-initiated efforts.
- Stay with the group and the group process; help the group process difficult emotions and work through the emotions, rather than trying to cover all the content.

Logistical Facilitation Tips

- *Manage Time Carefully:* Lengthy and unproductive discussions tend to frustrate everyone, so try to remain on task with your facilitation. During your initial overview of the session, give participants an idea of what will be covered and a general idea about how long the session will last. Be sure to stay as close to these time periods as possible. If necessary, appoint a timekeeper to help keep you on task. Doing this also helps with the "buy in" process. However, if an emotional issue is raised, be prepared to renegotiate time allocations in order to address the issue.
- *Check in with Participants:* Throughout your training session, "check in" with participants to see how they are feeling about the material covered and the session in general. Check-ins can be done shortly after the beginning of the session (after the introduction), during the middle of a session, and at the end of the session. If the training session is delivered over the course of multiple days, check in with participants at the start and end of each day. Assess their

comfort levels with the material, as well as assure them of your interest in their success in the course and the session's overall learning outcomes.

- *Use Journals:* Provide journals for participants or encourage them to bring their own to jot down notes during the session or use as work space to complete the individual and group exercises; many of the exercises require paper to complete.

- *Have Fun:* During sessions longer than an hour or so, use Koosh balls, stress balls, squishy balls, Play-Doh, pipe cleaners, foam dice, or other "quiet" playful objects to help create a relaxed, stress-free environment. Because discussions are typically left-brained activities, using objects, which use the right side of the brain, can help enhance participant creativity and involvement and make the experience more enjoyable. In addition to being used as stress relievers in a session, use of objects speaks to diverse learning styles. Objects can also be used in group games as well as group and paired selection exercises. Finally, consider ways to engage multiple senses; scented markers can be used to help create a fun and relaxed environment and playing soft music during breaks and reflection times may keep things relaxed. However, be sure to have a few unscented markers available for participants with sensitivities and make sure the music is appropriate.

PART TWO: Advice Chapters

The chapters in this section are written by expert facilitators. Each chapter focuses on a particular element relevant to facilitating a session about leading in a context of difference. Below are summaries of each chapter:

Handling Difficult Conversations in the Classroom
by Terrell L. Strayhorn

The focus of this chapter is handling difficult conversations in the classroom. The challenges and opportunities that face those who aspire to manage and participate in difficult conversations are discussed. The work of cultural studies in general and a social definition of culture in particular is addressed.

Keywords: Difficult conversations, culture, cultural studies, courageous conversations, cross-cultural misunderstandings, challenge and support, power dynamics, silence and voice, civility.

Key Points

- Culture is a description of a particular way of life, which expresses certain meanings and values not only in art and learning but also in institutions and ordinary behavior.
- In many ways, leading across differences requires one to be a cultural anthropologist who pays attention to the range of voices that are often silenced and unheard, as well as the tapestry of meanings that are often misunderstood.
- Challenges refer to encounters with new situations, stimuli for growth and development, and factors that may inhibit communication.

- Supports, on the other hand, refer to aspects of the material environment that provide the information needed to manage difficult dialogues; this can be thought of as cognitive support.
- Power *powerfully* influences the nature of dialogue. Facilitators are encouraged to think of ways to share the responsibility of teaching and learning with students when handling difficult conversations.
- The alternative to voicing one's experiences is silence. And silence is a dangerous weapon.
- Shouting differences without voicing commonalities is like throwing the cart before the horse; neither approach is likely to move very far.

Teaching Inclusion by Example and Experience
by Bernardo M. Ferdman

This chapter focuses on understanding what inclusion is—both for individuals and groups.

Keywords: Inclusion, inclusive learning environment, experience of inclusion, teaching inclusion, inclusive behavior, authority dynamics, power and dynamics, language, comfort

Key Points

- Diversity challenges leaders not only to recognize, respect, and value differences, but also to pay special attention to inclusion.
- Inclusion involves both being fully ourselves and allowing others to be fully themselves in the context of engaging in common pursuits.
- For individuals, experiencing inclusion in a group or organization involves being fully part of the whole while retaining a sense of authenticity and uniqueness.
- Inclusive organizations and groups are more likely to be effective, and groups will function well when their members have a sense that they are valued and can be open about their social identities.
- Leaders who are skilled at behaving inclusively and fostering inclusion in their organizations should be more likely to achieve better results and to be more successful in their roles.
- Inclusion can only be taught through experience. If we have not ourselves experienced what it means to be inclusive and to be included, we are less likely to be able to demonstrate inclusive leadership.

- Teaching inclusion requires addressing issues in the moment, as they arise, in the context of an overall plan.

- One of the best ways for participants to learn how to behave and to lead inclusively is to practice inclusion in the classroom and to learn what inclusion can be through example.

- To foster inclusion, it is important that facilitators/teachers remain aware of authority dynamics and not take responsibility for choices that participants need to make or fall into the trap of becoming paternalistic or authoritarian, even if this seems to be what participants might be more comfortable and/or familiar with.

- As groups learn and work together, developing an inclusive learning environment includes the capacity to reflect on process, both individually and collectively.

Building Safe Learning Environments by Laurien Alexandre

This chapter discusses how to create safe learning environments, in which individuals belonging to highly diverse identity groups feel comfortable expressing and exploring issues of race, class, gender, and other faultlines. The most important element that contributes to a safe learning culture is the establishing of a culture of equality through respectful information sharing and mutual growing that empowers all involved.

Keywords: safe learning community, faultlines, culture of equality, relational practice, learner centered, positionality, unconditional positive regard

Key Points

This chapter describes basic behaviors that facilitate safe learning environments and good discussion, including the following:

- Try to listen carefully and be respectful of one another's humanity.
- Try not to make a quick judgment.
- Try to prevent dominant consensus from silencing numerical minority dissent (regardless of your own convictions); give voice to all.
- Utilize dialogue strategies that provide space for voice, silence, and listening.
- Hold all participants in positive regard and value their contributions.
- Model how to have discussions about " isms" without making it personal.

- Intervene appropriately when offensive things are being said without pushing the offender into a corner.
- Don't pretend to know everything; allow for vulnerability.
- Support ways of learning together by common readings, shared experiences, and learner-initiated efforts.

Using Film to Illustrate Different Perspectives by Clemson Turregano and Belinda B. McFeeters

This chapter discusses ways in which facilitators might use film to illustrate or make more "real" the experiences of difference.

Keywords: film, visual media, reframe, purposeful viewing, cinema

Key Points
- Even though various theoretical perspectives suggest that people learn in many different ways, often trainers and those who teach others fail to take this into account when trying to reach their audiences in the classroom and other venues.
- Film offers insights to behavior, context, and a sensory understanding that is difficult to obtain from a textbook or lecture.
- Film should be used to role model or illustrate differences, bringing in a different medium to demonstrate a different view of a theory or a topic.
- The ability to reframe, to explore a position from multiple perspectives, is a teaching method often used in organizational and management education.
- When it comes to eliminating resistance and stereotypes among diverse individuals, using film is another useful and non-threatening method to consider.
- The key that turns entertainment into a foundation for dialogue and learning is referred to as *purposeful viewing*, which means to watch the film with a goal in mind.
- Using purposeful viewing, participants can key into leadership behaviors that are both positive and negative. They can reflect on their own reactions to those behaviors and whether the behaviors are conducive to effective leadership in a context of difference.

- Viewing good film teaches us the real truth about how people think, act, and dream, therefore gaining a good understanding about what makes people tick.
- Choose films that are relevant to the topic and portray the topic differently than a normal case study and in a much livelier manner than a book.

Assessing Leadership Across Differences Sessions by Emily Hoole

This chapter provides information about how to develop and implement an assessment process that enhances the use of the materials in the casebook and this Facilitator's Guide, and informs administrative decisions such as assigning grades.

Keywords: assessment, learning and development, data for improvement, data for decisions/judgment, learning objectives, knowledge-based objectives, developmental objectives, Bloom's Taxonomy, affective objectives, selective response, constructed response, behavioral assessment, bias

Key Points

- Ways in which assessment data might be used include to inform decisions regarding whether participants are learning what you expect; to inform efforts to improve learning and development; to understand the progress of a group of participants and to determine whether instructional changes are necessary to achieve the goals of the program; to assign individual grades; and to determine the long-term effects of the program.
- Using data to diagnose learning preferences and needs, to measure aptitude, and/or to monitor progress are improvement-related uses.
- Data for decisions/judgments would be used to assign grades, rate performance, or measure instructional effectiveness.
- Clear objectives need to be written prior to the development of the instructional plan.
- Be sure that the objectives you seek and the instructional design you plan to use are tightly coupled. The objectives can be thought of as the intended outcomes, whereas the assessment data you collect later are the actual outcomes.
- Affective objectives are related to emotions, feelings, and beliefs.
- Bias occurs when participants of different groups (gender, race, ethnicity, social identity group) are either disadvantaged or advantaged in responding to certain items, leading to skewed responses.

Handling Difficult Conversations in the Classroom

Terrell L. Strayhorn

The focus of this chapter is handling difficult conversations in the classroom. Specifically, I address the challenges and opportunities that face those who aspire to manage and participate in difficult conversations. Central to this discussion is the work of cultural studies in general and a social definition of culture in particular. In this chapter, I use an inclusive social definition of culture whereby "culture is a description of a particular way of life, which expresses certain meanings and values not only in art and learning but also in institutions and ordinary behavior [sic]" (Williams, 2006, p. 32). Analysis of culture, then, is an activity aimed at clarifying the meanings and values implicit in one's ways of life; understanding the meanings that individuals attach to experiences; unraveling the complex interplay between social markers (for example, class), social locations (for example, gender or race), and ascribed meanings; articulating how particular meanings become embedded in everyday lives; and tracking the production, circulation, and consumption of meanings (Halle, Kurtz-Costes, & Mahoney, 1997). In many ways, leading across differences requires one to be a cultural anthropologist who, through cultural excavations of self and others, pays attention to the range of voices that are often silenced and unheard, as well as the tapestry of meanings that are often misunderstood.

CROSS-CULTURAL (MIS)UNDERSTANDINGS

Tensions that emerge when leading across differences tend to emanate from cross-cultural misunderstandings, conflicting cultural practices, contradictory networks of meanings, and the inability or unwillingness to engage "the other" in difficult dialogues or courageous conversations. For example, one must be sensitive to the cultural values assumed or implied in statements like "Women should be leaders," when discussing the role of women in leadership. Those from cultures where the role of women is to follow rather than lead may struggle to understand perspectives that differ so markedly from their own. As an instructor, you have to monitor yourself as well as the participants in your class for these potential barriers to understanding. In the following paragraphs, I describe each type of barrier, provide an example, and offer ideas for how to address the situation.

Cross-cultural misunderstandings occur for several reasons. First, cross-cultural misunderstandings arise because of the varied, and often incongruent, ways of thinking and meaning making that distinguish one group from the other. When an individual is confronted by networks of meanings that differ significantly from one's own, cognitive dissonance—the consequence of confronting a situation or problem that requires skills or meaning making structures different from those currently held (Baxter Magolda, 1998)—or culture shock may occur unless he or she is supported in ways that enable him or her to acquire and enact complex sensitivities and advanced forms of reasoning. Disequilibrium can be balanced by various supports, including progressively challenging tasks that foster one's mastery of requisite knowledge and skills, prolonged exposure to new and different ways that catalyze the development of coping strategies or resistance, and highly trained facilitators who strike a balance between the difficulty and the direction of dialogues. For example, as a child at home, I was taught to "never look adults directly in the eye or call them by their first names," as a way of signifying respect. So you can imagine my surprise (and discomfort) when my third-grade teacher complained that I failed to "look at [her] when spoken to" and my eleventh-grade teacher asked me to call her "Ruth, please." Working across differences can be complicated by contradictory cultural beliefs. As an instructor you want to foster and manage cultural disequilibrium among participants. One way to do this is to role model talking about it from your own experience—to use yourself and your experience as a teaching tool.

Whereas culture is concerned with the production, circulation, and consumption of meanings, and different meanings can be assigned to the same object as illustrated above (text, event, custom), meaning making is a fertile site for struggle and negotiation, resistance and incorporation (Storey, 2007). This is the second reason why cross-cultural misunderstandings emerge. For instance, although patting a young lad on the crown of his head might appear to be benevolent and benign to some, what it means to others (for example, those from Thailand or Laos consider it rude for strangers to touch the "home of one's spirit" [for more, see Jandt, 2007]) and the struggle over its meanings leaves room for debate, exploration, and interpretation. And it is this degree of freedom in interpretation that leads to dissent and lack of understanding. It is not the incident that matters; an isolated event rarely issues its own meaning. Rather, the incident is made to signify something, and it is how and why the event is made meaningful that matters most. By fixing a critical gaze on meaning making, instructors and students can more easily navigate through tensions that often stymie difficult dialogues in the classroom, as well as identify the key issues presented in the cases in the *Leading Across Differences* (LAD) casebook. One way to address this in a classroom setting is by articulating and honoring different interpretations and by discussing the importance of narrating actions; explaining one's perspective and intentions. The hidden and assumed meanings of action may not be shared generally among groups of people.

Using Sanford's (1962) notions of *challenge* and *support* as an organizing framework, the following section shifts the focus of the chapter toward the problems and potential solutions for handling difficult conversations in the classroom. Consonant with Sanford's understandings, I define challenges as encounters with new situations, stimuli for growth and development, and factors that may inhibit communication. Supports, on the other hand, refer to aspects of the material environment that provide the information needed to manage difficult dialogues; this can be thought of as cognitive support. Given the emotional nature of LAD, support here may also include emotional support and opportunities for introspection and for sharing within safe circles.

CHALLENGES TO HANDLING DIFFICULT DIALOGUES

There are several challenges that, if unconsidered, may inhibit one's ability to facilitate difficult dialogues in the classroom, including power (and its corollary "agency"), silence (and its audible twin "voice"), and the essentialism of differences. I address each of these below.

Power and Agency

Elsewhere I outline an integrated social justice framework (Strayhorn & Hirt, 2008) consisting of six key elements; the first of these is power. Power refers to the often unseen, insidious forces that fuel the marginalization of some and the emancipation and proclamation of others. Power can be a tool for increasing polarization or for bridging differences. Power in a context of difference often results, intentionally or not, in the daily injustices (microinequities) that render some people invisible (Ellison, 1952), disempowered, and unacceptably different (Atkinson, 2007), as well as the systemic and structural inequalities that give rise to and reinforce persistent sociocultural differences (Storey, 1999). Thus, power, unbridled, can either promote or prevent difficult dialogues; in the way of an old proverb, *power giveth and taketh away*. As an instructor, you are invariably in a powerful position and in a position to monitor and influence the power dynamics in the classroom.

Power dynamics exist between teachers and students, whites and minorities, men and women, managers and workers. These dynamics are established and reinforced by systemic and institutional policies around assessment/evaluation, harassment, and hiring/firing, to name a few, but also through social relations (such as gender roles) and cultural practices (for example, deference). For difficult dialogues to proceed constructively, environments must be safe, sanctioned spaces in which participants are encouraged to pursue truth, through free inquiry, wherever the path may lead (see the chapter in this guide, "Building Safe Learning Environments," for more information). Similarly, classrooms must be structured in ways that place *power-full* voices (teachers, majority groups) on the same plane as *small voices* (students, minority groups [for more, see Atkinson, 2007]), where each is both producer and recipient of conversation. Instructors must also acknowledge that ingrained power dynamics do not shift quickly or easily—acknowledging the differences and discussing them may be as close as one can get to leveling the plane. To illustrate this complex issue, consider the following anecdote, drawn from my teaching journal, which summarizes an incident that took place in my classroom two years ago:

> It's Wednesday and we had a GREAT discussion in class tonight. Great? No, powerfully transformative. We were talking about social justice. Students read several authors in preparation for class, including a short piece by Aristotle titled *Politics*, which talks about societies composed of rulers and subjects. Additionally, students were asked to attend a guest lecture by Sistah Souljah. I began the lesson by sharing my own frustrations with the various perspectives proffered by authors, particularly Sistah Souljah's soliloquy that seemed to demonize everything "Black and male." Then, I paused for response ... for conversation. As [said student] spoke, I stepped to the margin of the classroom; watching and listening to students engage each other in a difficult conversation about race and racism, power and oppression, the historical amnesia of America, and even their own personal histories. Five students cried. Three spoke loudly. Three "came out" as gay or lesbian. One male admitted to being a "free spirit" who enjoys "wearing dresses." What happened tonight was nothing short of magical—the magic that happens when students feel free to dialogue, safe and respected by their professor and peers, and when the professor dares to move from being the "sage on the stage" to being a "guide on the side."

While anecdotal in nature, this example illustrates several points that may be useful to facilitators, as well as suggests specific strategies that facilitators can use to handle difficult conversation. First, facilitators are encouraged to share a bit of themselves with students. By sharing my own frustrations with students, I allowed them to see me a *real* person with opinions, emotions, and feelings—not just a professor. Second, in addition to the cases in the casebook, facilitators might use historical or current events, speakers, or readings like the short piece by Aristotle to initiate conversations about difficult issues; we will return to this point later in the chapter. Third, facilitators should not be afraid to stand aside silently when students engage one another in difficult conversations. Realize, however, that in an emotionally charged atmosphere, the facilitator may need to take a more active role.

Power *powerfully* influences the nature of dialogue. Facilitators are encouraged to think of ways to share the responsibility of teaching and learning with students when handling difficult conversations. Journaling, oral presentations, and guiding from the sidelines may be useful strategies to employ, thereby giving agency to students to participate actively in meaning making. When analyzing *LAD* cases, students and educators should also pay attention to the position, values, and perspectives of those making decisions and those affected by decisions. Are these groups the same? How might race, gender, or other social markers color the experiences of those involved? Who is [dis]empowered? And how might one exercise agency despite adversity? One way to dismantle power that privileges one, while subjugating another, is to exercise one's agency by giving *voice* to one's own experiences, the experiences of those who speak with *small voices*, or the experiences of those who cannot speak for themselves in difficult conversations.

I mention my teaching journal above. Journaling is one way I can pay attention to my responses in the classroom and make sense of my experience. It also helps me role model for participants a reflective practice, which can be a valuable skill for leaders. My approach to journaling involves the following: (a) record the date and time of my reflection, (b) record the date and time of the class about which I am journaling, (c) recall and describe the class setting, including participants (Who was there?), (d) describe the events chronologically (What happened?), (e) highlight my role as instructor and that of my students, and (f) explain how I felt about the classroom experience. Facilitators of difficult conversations might use a similar approach when journaling about their experiences.

Silence and Voice

The alternative to voicing one's experiences is silence. And silence is a dangerous weapon. As King and Schneider aptly said: "When we refuse to talk about [something], the value of [it] increases on the black market of linguistic transactions" (1999, p. 131). In other words, silence is both seductive and complicitous. On the one hand, it begs attention and exploration no matter how unprepared one may be for what lies beneath. The other problem with silence is that it leaves or makes room for uninterrupted lessons of intolerance and misunderstandings. Thus, students are encouraged to exercise their agency by "speaking up" across differences, and not let the scream of silence persist in complicity. Facilitators, too, should work to [co]create conditions that engender active participation in conversations (Kuh, Schuh, Whitt, & Associates, 1991). Silence may suggest acceptance or agreement when, in fact, there is none—silence may reflect a lack of security or willingness to share one's perspective. As an instructor, you should encourage, but never force, someone to share his or her perspective. If there is a pause in the conversation, it may be worth talking about the silence. Is it agreement? A lack of interest? A lack of safety?

Essentialism of Differences

A third challenge facing those who handle difficult dialogues in the classroom is what I refer to as the essentialism of differences. That is, all too often conversations about diversity and leadership become polarized into unfettered political debates about fixed differences and those conditioned by one's social locations (such as gender), environments, and individual choices without even a passing glance at that which we share in common. Rarely, if ever, are such conversations productive, let alone comfortable and civil. Shouting differences without voicing commonalities is like throwing the cart before the horse; neither approach is likely to move very far. Instead, facilitators and students would do well to emphasize differences, such as those raised in the LAD cases, while identifying times at which there may be room for cooperation or common cultural understandings.

One caveat, however, is needed. Practicing civility should neither require leaving unspoken things that would interrupt normative discourses or challenge hidden and offensive assumptions, nor silence the voice of those who may speak the unpleasant, raise unpopular questions, or utter that which we would rather forget. This I refer to as the paradox of civility—that it can, at its worst, perpetuate the very social pathologies and perspectives that make mutual respect impossible and, at its best, represent one of the only panaceas for the "isms" that undermine community. Indeed, civility should never supplant candor and honesty. All too often, to avoid discomfort and untamed emotions, we succumb to the normalizing force of civility, sticking to safer, less difficult, usually less fruitful, dialogues. Like others (DePalma, 2007; Mankiller & Wallis, 1993), I see discomfort, righteous indignation, and civil disobedience as powerful and necessary conditions for leading and learning across differences, for transforming difficult dialogues into plausible solutions. It has been said that beautiful diamonds only come from subjecting impure carbon to very high temperatures under very high pressure; similar wisdom can be used, at times, when handling difficult conversations. To foster honest civility, instructors might allow for multiple truths or clarify that students' perspectives are uniquely their own without demanding unanimous consensus.

SUPPORTS FOR HANDLING DIFFICULT DIALOGUES

While the challenges mentioned above are formidable, there are a number of supports available to those who are charged with, or inclined toward, handling difficult dialogues in the classroom. A few of these include cases, texts, and multiple forms of media.

Cases are powerful tools for exposing learners to important, uncomfortable, or unfamiliar situations. Cases can also give voice in an unprecedented way to silenced populations by effectively shifting the emphasis from the individual to the actors in the case, from the specific to the general. Cases offer an entry point, an invitation, to a conversation about difference. Participants can use the opportunity to talk about their own experiences or use the cases as the focus and have a more detached conversation.

Texts are powerful tools for speaking the unspeakable through stories and songs, without placing students, trainees, or the instructor in harm's way. By fixing our critical gaze on characters, contexts, and the animation of leading across differences, written texts can illuminate thorny issues such as racism, sexism, and discrimination; present multiple, even unpopular, perspectives on a single debate; and accord readers an opportunity to think before speaking. This is often difficult, if not impossible, when facilitating "real time" dialogues in classroom and corporate settings without such tools. Many of the texts listed in the references section serve as useful heuristics.

Finally, various forms of media may also be helpful to facilitate difficult dialogues. Media is a dominant means for [re]producing, circulating, and enabling the consumption of cultural meanings. Indeed, it is a powerful voice. Although it can be uncomfortable to raise questions about thorny issues such as race, class, politics, religion, and sexuality in educational and corporate settings, media serves as a powerful tool for giving voice to our silenced fears, as music, film, and art allow us to speak the unspeakable without uttering a word. Educators are encouraged to consider ways in which the resources listed both throughout this chapter and at the end of this guide, combined with the LAD cases, can be marshaled to handle difficult conversations in the classroom. You may want to read the chapter about using film in the classroom and building safe learning environments in tandem with the cases in classes.

CONCLUSION

Armed with the information included in this chapter, plus the arsenal of information provided in the *Leading Across Differences* casebook, individuals can explore how people craft productive responses to uneasy questions, negotiate their social identities in various contexts, and overcome emotions to speak the unspeakable. Keep in mind that the issues and explanations provided in this chapter were designed to render the complex, simple, realizing that a degree of specificity is lost in the process. Rather than an authoritative treatment on this subject, the chapter was designed to provide a starting place for those who need assistance with handling difficult conversations in the classroom.

Teaching Inclusion by Example and Experience: Creating an Inclusive Learning Environment

Bernardo M. Ferdman

A key element of leadership is creating, sustaining, and enhancing the conditions that will encourage and allow people to do their best. Diversity challenges leaders not only to recognize, respect, and value differences, but also to pay special attention to inclusion. This requires understanding what inclusion is—for both individuals and groups—and supporting the development and manifestation of inclusive behaviors and practices. In its most general sense, inclusion involves both being fully ourselves and allowing others to be fully themselves in the context of engaging in common pursuits. It means collaborating in a way in which all parties can be fully engaged and subsumed, and yet, paradoxically, at the same time believe that they have not compromised, hidden, or given up any part of themselves. Thus, for individuals, experiencing inclusion in a group or organization involves being fully part of the whole while retaining a sense of authenticity and uniqueness.

Inclusion is especially important for leaders and managers—who have a key responsibility to help create and sustain the conditions that foster inclusion in groups and organizations (Wasserman, Gallegos, & Ferdman, 2008). Given growing evidence that inclusive organizations and groups are more likely to be effective (see Brickson, 2000; Cox, 2001; Creed & Scully, 2000; Davidson, 1999; Ferdman & Davidson, 2002; Gasorek, 2000; Gilbert & Ivancevich, 2000; Hyter & Turnock, 2005; Miller & Katz, 2002; Mor-Barak, 2005), as well as the higher likelihood that groups will function well when their members have a sense that they are valued and can be open about their social identities (Bowen & Blackmon, 2003; Ely & Thomas, 2001), leaders who are skilled at behaving inclusively and fostering inclusion in their organizations should be more likely to achieve better results and to be more successful in their roles. An inclusive work group is more likely to take advantage of its diversity and therefore have more resources and options available to achieve success (Avigdor, Braun, Konkin, Kuzmycz, & Ferdman, 2007).

A key to this process is the experience of inclusion. The *experience of inclusion* is "individuals' perception of the extent to which they feel safe, trusted, accepted, respected, supported, valued, fulfilled, engaged, and authentic in their working environment, both as individuals and as members of particular identity groups" (Ferdman, Barrera, Allen, & Vuong, 2009)—in short, the psychological sense on the part of individuals that indeed they are being included. When an individual experiences inclusion, she or he feels fully present and involved, believes that others recognize and appreciate his or her contributions, and feels both safe and open about his or her social identities. In this conceptualization, components of the experience of inclusion in work groups include involvement and engagement in the work group, the ability to be heard and to influence decision making, the feeling of being valued, a sense of authenticity or being able to bring one's whole self to work, and the sense that diversity is recognized, attended to, and honored (Ferdman, Barrera, Allen, & Vuong, 2009).

In this chapter I describe how to teach inclusion and how to create an inclusive learning environment in which the experience of inclusion and inclusive behavior are encouraged and maximized. An inclusive learning environment is desirable and important because it empowers learners, it energizes people, it promotes engagement, collaboration, and co-creation, and it models and allows leaders to practice what they should do and how they should behave. Most importantly, participants in an inclusive learning environment both experience inclusion themselves and learn how to help others experience inclusion.

I believe inclusion can only be taught through experience. If we have not experienced what it means to be inclusive and to be included, we are less likely to be able to demonstrate inclusive leadership. To help develop leaders who are skilled at inclusion, facilitators and teachers must begin with themselves and, through modeling and facilitation, help create an inclusive learning environment that encourages participants to engage in and learn about inclusive behavior consciously and deliberately, so that they can later transfer and apply that learning and those behaviors to their leadership practice. The key to this for the instructor is to model inclusive leadership, including infusing inclusion as a core element of course process and design.

Fostering an inclusive learning environment can be difficult because it is not necessarily what people are used to. It is challenging as a teacher or facilitator to relinquish control and/or predictability, and it requires much attention, skill, passion, as well as continuous learning and just-in-time design. For students, it is difficult because often their expectations regarding their own roles and that of the teacher can be challenged. To build and maintain an inclusive learning environment, one cannot be on automatic! It takes a lot of focus, energy, and emotional investment.

At the same time, teaching inclusion by practicing it can be exciting and energizing, because it permits learning in and from the moment, and, when successful, can be quite rewarding in itself. Teaching inclusion requires addressing issues in the moment, as they arise, in the context of an overall plan. It requires being aware of and capitalizing on here-and-now dynamics and possibilities, as well as wholeheartedly engaging with students and treating them as full learning partners. Because inclusion is a practice that is manifested and becomes real only in everyday interactions (albeit in a group and intergroup context, of course), teaching inclusion and doing so inclusively provides a medium particularly well-suited for learners to develop essential leadership skills.

INCLUSIVE BEHAVIOR AND PRACTICES

Inclusive behavior involves the actions and practices that foster the experience of inclusion, and has to do both with what we do ourselves and what others do to and with us (Ferdman, Barrera, Allen, & Vuong, 2009). Inclusive group- and organizational-level practices also help create and maintain a culture of inclusion (Ferdman, Barrera, Allen, & Vuong, 2009; Holvino, Ferdman, and Merrill-Sands, 2004; Mor-Barak, 2005; Wasserman, Gallegos, & Ferdman, 2008). In their measure of inclusive behavior—which addresses both one's own behavior and that of members of one's work group—Ferdman, Barrera, Allen, & Vuong (2009) include the categories of creating safety, acknowledging others, proactively and constructively addressing conflict and differences, being able and willing to learn, having and using one's voice, and fostering representation.

Recently, the Institute for Inclusion (www.instituteforinclusion.org), an organization founded to promote the value and practice of inclusion, has developed a list suggesting inclusive behaviors that everyone in an organization can do, those that leaders—especially those in positions of authority—should practice, and inclusive practices for organizations (Ferdman, Katz, Letchinger, & Thompson, 2009). The Institute's list of behaviors "for all" focuses on the following broad categories: acknowledging, connecting, and engaging with other people; listening skillfully and deeply; being transparent, speaking up, and sharing information, as well as encouraging a broad range of others to do so; being curious and open to alternative views and possibilities; becoming "comfortable with discomfort"; becoming more reflective and self-aware; learning from and being open to the influence of others; respecting others and being fair; and focusing on and working on behalf of the collective in an interdependent manner (Ferdman, Katz, Letchinger, & Thompson, 2009).

According to the Institute's list (Ferdman, Katz, Letchinger, & Thompson, 2009), in addition to these behaviors, leaders have further responsibilities with regard to supporting an inclusive culture. The categories of inclusive behaviors for leaders include the following: building accountability for oneself and others with regard to inclusion; fostering and inviting connection and dialogue; being authentic and bringing all of one's self to work, and allowing and encouraging others to do so; fostering transparency, particularly in decision making; reframing and connecting with "resistance"; explicitly connecting inclusion to collective goals; and speaking up about inclusion.

Organizational practices for inclusion listed by the Institute (Ferdman, Katz, Letchinger, & Thompson, 2009) include building a climate of "respect, fairness, justice, and equity"; making sure that there is an underlying framework for developing and assessing organizational policies and practices with regard to inclusion, and that inclusion is integrated systemically throughout the organization; supporting the development of multicultural competencies for individuals and groups; clarifying the organization's approach to social responsibility; fostering transparency, participation, and openness, as well as teamwork; making sure that diversity is present and valued; and engaging in and valuing ongoing learning and continuous development. To foster an inclusive learning environment, teachers and facilitators must learn about, incorporate, and foster these practices for themselves and others in the classroom.

INCLUSION IN THE CLASSROOM

In teaching, I have found that one of the best ways for students to learn how to behave and to lead inclusively is to practice inclusion in the classroom and to learn what inclusion can be through example. My experience comes, in part, from teaching a graduate-level course on diversity in organizations for the last twenty-two years (see http://bernardoferdman.org/Articles/ORG7330_Spring_2009_syllabus.pdf for the latest version of the course syllabus; an adapted version is available in the online Instructor's Guide for the casebook). I also conduct workshops on diversity and inclusion and related topics for a variety of audiences, including managers and executives. My graduate course combines exposure to theory, practice, and research on diversity and inclusion, with a great deal of attention to creating a classroom climate that encourages individual and collective self-reflection. For example, students work on semester-long field-work group projects in which they must both learn about diversity in an organization of their choice and apply their learning to their own group. They are also required to write weekly reflections that not only address their readings, but also apply insights and perspectives gained from those readings to their class and field-work group experiences.

Setting Expectations and Welcoming Everyone

The first step for instructors or facilitators in the process of teaching inclusion is to be clear about their goals—both for themselves and for the group. To be able to create an inclusive learning environment, I have to be willing to reveal much about myself and to behave in an inclusive way, even before the course begins. As I have described elsewhere (Ferdman, 2007a, 2007b), inclusion starts with knowing oneself. It is only when I can be clear about who I am, in a way that is personally meaningful, and I am open to sharing of myself with others, that I can include myself, as well as more fully include others. I also need to make sure that I am willing and able to pay attention to my own process and reactions: How skilled am I at listening? How open am I to feedback and other input? How proficient am I in engaging in difficult conversations (Stone, Patton, & Heen, 1999)? How willing am I to develop these skills further? In this sense, a self-check and grounding are critical foundations for teaching inclusion.

Building an inclusive learning environment means being clear, explicit, and intentional—first with myself and then with students or participants—about the reasons for various choices in the course design, and to be prepared to explain these reasons when asked. In many cases, it may require some flexibility and adaptation after learning how my choices are experienced by students. The challenge is balancing one's responsibility for envisioning the course as a whole and designing it in light of the objectives with the understanding that participants always come in with their own objectives, experiences, and perspectives. It is important to provide ways to give voice to, to engage with, and to respond to the wisdom, experience, and goals that students bring and to incorporate these into the course's process and design.

Whether or not I am willing or able to modify particular components based on student input, what I have learned is that it is important to be forthright and truthful with students and to give them the information that they need and request while trusting them to make their own informed choices. Primarily, it is important to engage with students as fellow learners; indeed, I tell students at the outset, in framing my philosophy for the course, that I will be learning along with them, and that part of how I judge the success of the course is based on whether I, too, grow and learn. All too often, teachers and facilitators—especially in educational settings involving grades or other evaluations—take up their roles and are treated by students in ways that exaggerate their authority. To foster inclusion, it is important that teachers remain aware of authority dynamics and not take responsibility for choices that students need to make or fall into the trap of becoming paternalistic or authoritarian, even if this seems to be what students might be more comfortable and/or familiar with. At the same time, the teacher must be willing to appropriately take up his or her authority and responsibility to make suitable choices regarding course design and process.

I have found that one of the most powerful ways in which I signal my intention to be inclusive is in how I greet students or participants on the first day of class. Before formally starting, I make sure to go to each individual student at his or her seat, introduce myself and ask his or her name, shake his or her hand, and greet him or her genuinely and enthusiastically. Many students comment in their written reflections later that this is a very powerful experience for them, one that immediately tells them that this course will be different than others to which they are accustomed. Recently, when I conducted a six-hour workshop for managers, I had only been able to greet about two-thirds of the participants when the local host began to introduce me at the session start time. After I was introduced and given the floor, I asked the participants to bear with me while I finished saying hello to everyone.

Relatively early in the first session of my twelve-week course, I ask everyone to introduce him- or herself so as to encourage full participation, sharing, novelty (something about you that makes you unique, something about yourself that is new for everyone here), and voicing of everyone's hopes and expectations (one expectation you have for the course) right at the outset. In this way, everyone's voice is heard, with the goal of establishing a pattern and expectation of egalitarianism, participation, and sharing. Similarly, in every subsequent session I share the agenda for the day, and always ask whether there is anything anyone needs to add, contribute, share, or ask. After introducing the course theme of diversity (and engaging students in that process), I also introduce myself in a relatively extensive way, going beyond professional details to say something about my life story, family, and background, and I encourage students to ask any questions about me that they may have. I proceed to answer the questions as straightforwardly and openly as I can. This conveys to students that I am open to sharing and that I will take up my role in a way that they are often not used to seeing in other faculty. The goal is to establish a learning partnership from the very first moment, while being explicit about that intention and expectation, and to model the way in which inclusive leaders respond to questions from followers. By humanizing myself and also giving voice to every participant, the stage is set to foster inclusion. A key component to this is being prepared and intentional and sharing with participants my thinking about what I am doing as I am doing it.

While extensive introductions may not be possible in shorter sessions—for example, a one-time two-hour workshop—I believe that some kind of check-in that allows everyone to connect and to bring his or her full presence into the room is important to set the stage for inclusion. This can involve quickly going around the room so that everyone's voice is heard, using short paired introductions, or employing other techniques that immediately engage and connect with everyone present, in a way that avoids ranking or judging and makes it clear that everyone's contribution is needed and valued.

Co-Constructing Norms for Learning

Inclusion needs to be defined in each situation and for each person (Ferdman & Davidson, 2002), and the psychological experience of inclusion is key. Because different people may think about inclusion differently and have different needs or desires for inclusion, the facilitator's or teacher's intent does not have equal effect. For this reason, it is important to co-construct the meaning and practice of inclusion in the particular situation at hand, with the people who are present. If participants can do this effectively, they will be able to set the stage to learn many other aspects of leading across differences.

In my own classroom, I do this very early in the semester, with a full session devoted to addressing safety, to learning about the process of dialogue, and to developing norms for the learning community. In my syllabus, I indicate that "the effectiveness of the course will hinge on how well students contribute to the creation and maintenance of an inclusive, dynamic, safe, and supportive learning community" (Ferdman, 2009, p. 4) and that I "expect that [students] will approach the class as a laboratory for practicing inclusive behaviors and experiencing their impact" (p. 5). This is manifested through a specific dialogue period in every class session, which students lead, beginning with the fourth class of the semester. In the second session, I spend quite a bit of time explaining the concept of dialogue, after facilitating one, as well as talking about safety and boundaries. Questions posed to the group in that first dialogue include the following: "What is the relevance of the skills of dialogue and of difficult conversations to diversity and inclusion—for you personally, for this course specifically, and for organizations more generally? How do you see yourself practicing and applying those skills in this group (right now and in the future)? What feelings do you have about doing this right here and right now?" In this way, students begin to learn simultaneously about the concept of dialogue and about experiential learning.

To establish norms, I ask students first to form into pairs and then into quartets, with the latter constituting groups that they will stay with throughout the semester, and to share highlights regarding partnerships that worked really well and what made those work. Then I ask them to share views in their groups regarding what they should do and how they should be together to create a positive learning environment throughout the semester and to come up with three to five guidelines to create an effective and positive learning partnership for themselves as a group. After groups share their guidelines, I review a set of learning community behaviors (Katz & Miller, 1996) for the class as a whole and ask each individual to visibly indicate his or her willingness to commit to these as collective norms for the semester. I then ask the class to come up with a confidentiality agreement that will meet the needs of everyone in the group and to which everyone will commit. These steps are grounded in the explicitly stated goal of clarifying what everyone needs individually and how the group needs to be to get the best from and to learn from each other.

Although it may not be feasible in groups that will meet for less time to go through these elaborate steps, the key is to establish clear and appropriate boundaries and norms, to include learners in that process in a way that gives everyone an opportunity to participate and to be heard, and to begin to model and to practice dialogue. It should be possible to do this in any learning setting.

Developing a Collective Understanding of Inclusion

As groups learn and work together, developing an inclusive learning environment includes the capacity to reflect on process, both individually and collectively. In my course on diversity, this is addressed with a variety of activities and assignments. The link among these is a focus on multiple levels of systems (individual, group, organization, social identity groups, society, etc.) and on mutual responsibility within and across levels. Part of leadership development involves being able to see the complexity of most situations (as well as to learn that any one person cannot see or understand everything).

To emphasize the importance of developing a personally and collectively meaningful vision of inclusion and to promote individuals' connection with the concept, I typically ask the groups with which I work to figure out what inclusion means to them, rather than simply presenting them with my definition. One example of how I do this is described in Ferdman (2004). A variation of that activity involves asking people working in pairs to do the following:

1. *Think about a specific time when you felt especially included and valued in a diverse organization or team, and others there did, too. You felt effective, valuable, successful, engaged, authentic, complete, proud, and ALIVE at work—you could be fully yourself AND contribute fully to your group and organization.*

2. *Share a brief story about that experience. What happened? What was it like? What did you feel?*

3. *Explore what it was that helped you to feel included. What did you do? What did others do? What did the organization and its leaders do?*

After the pairs talk, a debriefing conversation with the whole group focuses not only on the content of the paired interviews, but also on the experience of sharing and the energy that it released.

This type of activity and the ensuing conversations have the effect of making inclusion a shared theme for a group. This theme can then be explored in relation to any other topic or case that is discussed. Nevertheless, more powerful than conversation about external experiences and cases is the shared experience in the classroom. In the activity above, a key part of the learning has to do with reflecting on the experience of being heard in the moment and of engaging with someone who is genuinely interested in learning about what one has to say, without passing judgment or seeking to incorporate it into one's own frameworks or world views.

CHALLENGES AND DILEMMAS

Teaching and modeling inclusion, while desirable, are not easy. In seeking to do this over the years, I have encountered a number of challenges and dilemmas, and in the process have found some helpful ways to address these.

Power and Diversity

As mentioned earlier, issues of authority are quite important in teaching inclusion and in teaching inclusively. Being sensitive to, thoughtful about, and, ideally, explicit in dealing with power dynamics, especially when these relate to social identities—as they often do—is a critical part of one's role as a teacher or facilitator. Foldy, Rivard, and Buckley (2009), building on intergroup theory (Alderfer & Smith, 1982) and on the work of Ely and Thomas (2001), argue that learning in racially and ethnically diverse teams and groups is more likely when there is psychological safety (Edmonson, 1999); in such groups, safety is positively related to diversity only when group members feel "identity safety"—that people with their particular identity are not at risk and are welcome in the group—and this feeling is only likely, in turn, to the degree that the paradigm for difference in the group is one of integration and learning (Ely & Thomas, 2001). Traditional power dynamics make this difficult, and instructors or facilitators must pay special attention to how issues that arise are handled with regard to the learning frames that are fostered, how their own power is deployed, and how participants and their identity groups are empowered or disempowered. Because participants are being asked to attend to multiple kinds of differences in the material that they are learning about, it is also critical to attend to dynamics involving similar differences as they play out in the classroom. Encouraging and supporting students to learn about multiple identities (see, for example, Ferdman, 2003) and about privilege and subordination (see, for example, Davidson & Ferdman, 2002; Ely, 1995) can help with this process.

Instructors and facilitators must be particularly sensitive to how they deploy their power to evaluate, to judge, and to promote some ideas over others. In a learning setting, it is important to be able to guide learners toward certain ideas, and it may also be necessary in many cases to correct errors or to clarify concepts that may be fuzzy or even wrong. Yet how this is done can have profound impact on the degree to which the classroom is experienced as inclusive and the degree to which particular learners are willing to speak up.

Language

One of the challenges of learning about diversity and striving to be inclusive is that of dealing with stereotypes. Students—especially those coming in with the belief that any explicit attention to group differences or group identities is inappropriate—often struggle with how to find appropriate language with which to talk about differences tied to social identities without seeming to be prejudiced or to be engaged in stereotyping. One way to help begin to undo this knot is to address the dilemma directly, by discussing the paradox of individual and group perspectives on fairness (see, for example, Ferdman, 1997) and to support the group in finding ways that make sense and work for the participants. This can work best when there are multiple representatives of any given identity group present, and when they do not collude to hide intra-group diversity. By learning about the distinction between stereotypes—which are typically negative and are inappropriately applied to individuals—and cultural differences—which are typically based on research and observation and are not indiscriminately applied to individuals but rather are attempts to describe general patterns at the group level—students can begin to develop a vocabulary for talking about diversity in a way that is more descriptive and less judgmental.

A related aspect of language has to do with the tendency of many people to externalize their statements or to speak in the second person. By establishing the norm that participants should use "I" statements, as well as by modeling it, instructors can support the group members in learning to practice speaking authentically and for themselves. This is supported through the use of dialogue skills, including inquiry.

Related to this, to effectively learn about and across differences in an inclusive way, it is important to promote curiosity and the suspension of judgment. Certainly, the ground rules and focusing on learning community behavior is an important part of this. Even more important is that the instructor model this process at all times. For example, when students challenge aspects of the course, or try to change the parameters, or otherwise express their authority, it is important to model the behaviors that are being addressed in the course material.

In my own course, I emphasize the concepts of the experience cube (Bushe, 2001) and of the ladder of inference (for example, Noonan, 2007) as tools for separating data—including our observations, thoughts, feelings, and desires—from the interpretations and meaning that we give to those data, and the conclusions or judgments that we derive based on those interpretations. The key is to support the development of a shared language for processing both here-and-now events as well as other course material, including cases, in a way that is inclusive and gives equal opportunities to all present to engage and participate.

Comfort

Another challenge of inclusion has to do with the issue of comfort. In part, inclusion is about helping individuals to feel relatively more comfortable and safe, especially when they are members of groups that have been traditionally marginalized or subordinated. Yet, particularly in a developmental setting in which the goal is learning, the focus cannot and should not be on comfort but on growth and building competence. As in exercise, where the best results are obtained when we stretch, push ourselves, and practice, inclusive learning environments demand something of everyone. Of course, the challenge is finding the right point between being too comfortable and being stretched too far. Instructors need to be especially attuned to signals that this balance may be upset for particular individuals, or even for the group, and should be prepared to restore balance through appropriate interventions. These could include changing the format, speaking up, managing the speaking queue, asking individuals for their input, or asking appropriate questions and going around the whole room so that everyone has the opportunity to weigh in.

Part of managing this challenge is recognizing that conditions that are comfortable for one person may be less so for another, yet inclusion requires that everyone be equally (or at least equitably) uncomfortable. For example, not everyone is equally skilled at or able to speak up in a group, especially without formal turns.

Similarly, individuals have different levels of comfort with sharing their perspectives or their experiences. For this reason, part of the instructor/facilitator's role involves both addressing such differences explicitly, as well as encouraging people to stretch (although not too far) into areas of discomfort. For people who speak a lot, the learning edge may involve learning to listen first and waiting until others have spoken before chiming in. For those who are more prone to stay quiet, the learning edge may involve trying out the new behavior of speaking up sooner. The key is to encourage using the group as a supportive learning and practice space. In my own teaching practice, I try to make sure that there are multiple options for participation. Sometimes, for example, I will pose a question and go around the room. I also incorporate online dialogue forums, in which participants can give their input in writing and asynchronously.

Keeping It Fresh

Ultimately, the primary tool an instructor has for teaching inclusion is him- or herself. When I am open to new ideas, when I continue to learn and model that in the classroom, when I own my mistakes, and when I don't just talk about inclusion but practice it, I am more likely to be effective in fostering an inclusive learning environment and to support deeper learning about inclusive leadership and about leading across differences. Even when using exercises, activities, or cases that I have used dozens of times before, I am most effective when I approach the situation anew, in the sense that I am fully present, engaged with the particular group and individuals in front of me, and paying attention to the here-and-now dynamics and the needs and voices of the individuals in the room. By teaching in this way, I not only keep it fresh for students, but also for myself.

Building Safe Learning Environments

Laurien Alexandre

Thinking about safety in learning communities can take many different forms, from protection against violence in workplace teams to establishing norms for respectful classrooms to the realization of a space for interpersonal acceptance and growth. In this chapter, "safe" refers to learning environments in which individuals belonging to highly diverse identity groups feel comfortable expressing and exploring difference. Because so many societal and organizational factors set the context for relationships within a group, it is both difficult and undesirable to try to establish a one-size-fits-all set of practices that create safe and inclusive learning environments.

In this chapter I discuss ways in which one highly diverse learning community addresses safety around issues of race, class, gender, and other faultlines. For almost a decade, I have been the director of a U.S.-based doctoral program with approximately 130 full-time students. Forty percent are students of color, 60 percent are women, approximately 50 percent are fifty years of age or older, 5 percent are international students. The students are drawn from a wide range of professional sectors including education, nonprofit, government, and business, akin to the highly diverse teams found in workplaces and organizations worldwide. There are eight core faculty, five women and three men, four faculty are born outside of the United States, two are faculty of color, and two faculty members self-identify as gay or lesbian. This particular doctoral program is referred to as a hybrid blended model of face-to-face quarterly residencies and a vibrant virtual learning community between these meetings.

My belief is that some of the strategies practiced by this diverse group of students and faculty in an innovative U.S.-based doctoral community may be enlightening and, to some degree, transferable to other settings such as leadership development programs and in-depth training workshops in which individuals spend significant learning periods together over time. As an introductory caveat, because there are many books and articles written to date that identify steps for fostering dialogue across divides (for example, Public Conversations Project, 2004; Stone, Patton, & Heen, 1999) and facilitating communication across cross-cultural differences (Anti-Defamation League, 2004; Hannum & Weber, 2005), in this chapter I take the approach of basing my comments on the experiences of students and faculty and relating these practices to scholarly work.

Let's start with the obvious: When faculty and facilitators think about learning, they typically are focusing on teaching, placing emphasis on instructional objectives and materials, curriculum content, and syllabi sequence. Instructors typically think about what they want to teach based on their training and expertise. Of course, all of that is incredibly important, but it doesn't ensure that a learning community will be safe for expressing difference nor successful in preparing participants to thrive in a diverse climate. Focusing on the content, pacing, and sequencing of instruction only ensures that the content will be about difference. The process of building a safe learning community is perhaps even more paramount.

In preparation for this chapter, I asked the current students in the doctoral program what they identified as elements of a safe environment in which to discuss diversity and, if their doctoral program created such an environment, how that was accomplished. I also asked faculty what they did as facilitators of learning to build safe spaces. The responses were illuminating and highlight what safe learning environments mean to those involved. I have structured their comments around two categories: learning culture and faculty/facilitator roles.

LEARNING CULTURE

The nature of organizational culture has much to do with the ways in which intergroup dynamics are addressed, as has been discussed throughout the casebook and alluded to also in this Facilitator's Guide. With regard to the doctoral program in question, the culture strives to be one in which shared bonds are created, and attention is focused on learning how to be a learning community. Below I explore the elements that contribute to the learning culture and consider how these may be applicable to different learning settings.

Establishing a Culture of Equality

More than curricula, pedagogy, or learning outcomes, there is something essential about establishing a welcoming community that honors each individual into a culture of equality. This isn't meant to naively assume that all participants are the same. Clearly, there are students who are more or less prepared for intense study, more or less engaged in learning, and the like, just as in training programs there are participants more or less eager to engage. There are also authority differences and positional power relationships. Faculty have the responsibility to evaluate and pass judgment on participants' work. Facilitators in leadership development programs have the authority to present certification or notification of completion. And, of course, not all personalities work and play well together, a fact that we witness not only in formal learning communities but in virtually every organization and workplace. Yet, all this said, people within this learning community come together as equals, although having different roles and responsibilities. "Creating safety is a shared responsibility," writes one student. "Therefore, as a member of a particular cohort and of the larger doctoral [learning] community, I feel I must take responsibility for creating a welcoming and safe environment. I say this to say that creating a welcoming environment is a shared effort."

We try to orient our working together toward respectful information sharing and mutual growing that empowers all involved. The program is committed to the underlying belief that each and every community member has the ability and the right to succeed. That message is reiterated in many ways from the first day forward. The norms for respectful discourse are set in the first year—everyone has the right to speak, but no one is required to speak; everyone has the right to voice difference; and differences of opinion are presented with respect and grounded in scholarship and substantiated opinion, not pure emotion—and then continue throughout. In their casebook chapter on leadership practices, Ruderman, Glover, Chrobot-Mason, and Ernst discuss the importance of redundant systems and multiple practices that reinforce cross-group communication throughout an organization. The doctoral program strives to practice this redundancy and reinforcement consistently throughout, especially in the ways in which we treat the community members. Paramount in our thinking is what these adult learners need to feel safe, do their best, and achieve their goals.

One student noted, "The democratic organizational spirit and structure of the program create a container for safe learning, exploration, expression, conflict, and change. The concepts of democracy as freedom and education as a liberating force are strong and honored values within the faculty and student body. Obviously, the staff and students have worked effectively to create a sense of community and reasonable trust, both of which are critical in developing a safe learning space."

As the above comment indicates, much emphasis is placed on learning effectively together and creating a shared community identity. This means an emphasis on "relational practice" as discussed by Fletcher (2001) in terms of trust, mutuality, and empathy. Recognizing that the whole person comes to the learning community, honoring uniqueness and commonality is essential. Every effort is made by faculty and staff to welcome the whole person into the learning community. In our particular program, this takes many forms, from the nature of individual communication and care extended by faculty to unusual programmatic behaviors, such as inviting partners and spouses to attend class meetings. As another student noted, "You make each student feel like she or he is important. The faculty are 'present' when interacting with the students."

Practical Strategies to Create a Welcoming Organizational Spirit

- Be learner centered. Learn about and place the participants' learning goals at the core of facilitator/faculty efforts, staff practices, and/or management decisions.
- Invite and welcome newcomers into the community with warmth, honoring their uniqueness and offering opportunities for participants to get to know each other as whole persons from the outset.
- Create structures to support cohort-ness and collaborative learning opportunities, such as joint assignments and credit for peer collaboration.
- Create times for the community to have fun together, such as community-building activities with a sense of levity, laughter, and compassion.
- Create a track of activities for spouses and partners so that working adults, who already have too little time with families, can choose to bring their whole lives to the learning community.

Creating a Shared Identity Based on a Common Goal

Various chapters in the casebook discuss the importance of a shared identity that binds individuals from different social identity groups together—a common professional identity, for example, helps individuals feel part of the same group and resolve differences respectfully. As stated in her casebook chapter on social identity, Nkomo indicates that evoking a superordinate purpose "allows groups and individuals within the groups to recategorize themselves as belonging to a superordinate identity."

The highly emotional and challenging identity of being a doctoral student and becoming a scholar—with all of its disorienting dilemmas—becomes a strong force irrespective of students' professional identities, power positions, and social group identities. In many ways, it levels the playing field because all members of the community are learners, no matter what power and privilege their external social identities confer. This means that, whether a learner is a wealthy CEO, a Native American activist, an urban environmentalist, or a skilled professional, all come to the learning environment unsure of how they will fare, what the future holds, and they often lack confidence in their abilities as scholars. "Real-world" identity group memberships do not disappear. However, the strength of the students' desires to accomplish their goals coupled with the program's cohort structure, which requires peer (team) learning embedded within a non-competitive learning model, strengthens the commitment to a shared direction and common goal. In other contexts, focusing on an identity that everyone has in common can be the bridge.

The cohort model and small dialogue groups of eight to ten learners create a comfortable zone for learning together. As one student notes, "I think the smaller groups are more intimate, which encourages greater expression of thoughts and ideas." These comments reflect William Issacs' (1999) notion of dialogue, in which he suggests that the ability to conduct successful dialogue, what he refers to as the art of thinking together, is the ability to embrace different points of view—listening, respecting, suspending, and voicing. These are certainly abilities that let us learn across difference.

The challenge we face as faculty and facilitators—whether in formal classrooms or informal learning environments—is how to get highly motivated, task-oriented individuals to dialogue together for mutual benefit, rather than solely focus on their personal goals and successes. I fundamentally believe the answer rests with creating environments that support growth-in-relation. Within such environments, social identity faultlines can be understood and diminished so that triggering events, when they happen (and they will) don't shatter the bonds. In this program, learning is an active and interactive process of participating with highly motivated peer learners, not a process conducted in isolation and for self-gain. Peer collaboration is rewarded both in terms of formal credit and in terms of faculty support in the cohort discussions.

One of the preconditions for mutual growth-in-relation to happen is to eliminate as much competition between individuals in the learning environment as possible by making achievement of one's personal goals embedded in and enriched by the larger community's mission and purpose. Toward this goal, the program does not use a grading system. There are no evaluation curves that require one student to fail for another to succeed. As we tell students from the outset, the program faculty are committed to the success of every student who is willing to work hard. This is a rather unusual approach in formal education whereby grades take on a paramount importance. Not having a grading system takes the focus away from competition and the end product and places focus on the learning and the journey throughout. Of course, quality work is expected, narrative evaluations are given, and commencement credits are awarded but not compared. In less formal learning environments, there may be other ways to diminish the competition between individuals that would have a similar effect.

What our experience suggests it that even a doctoral program, often known as a highly competitive and individualistic endeavor where only 50 percent of those who enter will complete (National Council of Graduate Schools, 2008), provides the perfect opportunity to build a mutually empowering, task-oriented, interdependent learning community. Unfortunately, most doctoral programs in my opinion do exactly the opposite, creating isolated individuals competing against each other in a high-stakes game for faculty favors and personal recognition. National trends demonstrate that the results of such practices are high attrition numbers and, within those, many learners of difference—particularly women, students of color, and working adult students—lose out and leave (Lovitts, 2001; National Council of Graduate Schools, 2008). In some of the cases being shared in the casebook, participation in a learning community that cares about the whole person and nurtures mutually empowering learning allows for the opportunity of recategorization that can diminish separation and allow for mutuality, as discussed in a number of the casebook's chapters, as well as in the chapter by Ferdman in this Facilitator's Guide.

Practical Strategies for Building a Common Goal of Success for All Learners

- Diminish individual competition and reward collaboration.
- Strive to diminish much of the isolation of formal study. Encourage students to share their work within the cohort, post exemplars to help each other, and develop the skills of respectful scholarly discourse.
- Establish policies and practices that support the success of all participants, not just the top or bottom 10 percent.

Learning to Be a Learning Community

At the core of all these processes is the intentionality of learning to be a learning community. The "intent to learn" (Bentz & Shapiro; 1998, p. 163) is a powerful precondition for openness to go beyond one's existing boundaries in order to find out something about the other. There is a mystique that we learn alone in quiet rooms with mountains of books piled high on our desks or in formal classroom settings with an expert "sage on the stage" transmitting knowledge to a group of passive recipients. While there is truth in these images, they are not the whole story; in fact, neither of these images has much to do with learning that emerges within an inclusive learning community.

When asked, a number of our program's students focused on the learning that happens in the safe holding environment of their proseminar, which is a cohort-based "homeroom" that meets face-to-face and online and stays together throughout the time that students progress through the pre-candidacy years. This is the smallest and most intimate unit within the learners' world; in the proseminar, students know each other most deeply and fully and find mutual support and build individual resilience. While faculty facilitated, there is also a formal space created within the proseminar, called intervision, which is just for the students alone to discuss their growing and learning pains. The proseminar's format and focus change developmentally as the students mature over time into a respectful community of emergent scholars.

The structure of proseminar over the three pre-candidacy years strives to facilitate a safe environment for dialogue around sensitive issues. One student writes, "The first-year proseminar was extremely nurturing and also demonstrated the many ways in which knowledge is gained, perceived, and shared. The faculty member modeled the practice of appreciative inquiry, a way of learning that fosters a safe, respectful learning environment. She also helped us practice respectful engagement so that we grew to feel increasingly secure in allowing ourselves to be authentic." The second-year proseminar is anchored around students critiquing research articles that often explore controversial issues. A student writes, "The faculty member's nonjudgmental posture helped us appreciate differences around some difficult issues. His only requirement was that we think critically and begin to develop scholarly habits." The third-year proseminar builds on the learning community's maturation as a group as they begin to discuss their dissertation ideas. One student notes, "We can feel each other's growing comfort in the role of scholar-practitioner and researcher. Our growth has made us humble and confident at the same time. We are eager to attack the sensitive issues around leadership and difference, especially those that pertain to race, gender, class, inequity, privilege, and marginalization."

As the above suggests, the program is quite intentional in the ways it structures learning, the proseminar being just one example. Another is the use of certain methodologies to facilitate dialogue that provides a safe place for difference to be expressed. One of the more powerful strategies is the incorporation of "talking circles." The faculty member who most utilizes this is a highly experienced and skilled Native American scholar with background in human development. She describes the process in the following way: "The Native American tradition of the 'talking circle' encourages equality. Each person's talking is special and there are no interruptions from 'experts' or 'advice givers.' There is a lot of silence or quiet for reflection. This method creates an environment of safety. Everyone is required to do a lot of listening instead of the professor or several dominant students having the floor for most of the time. If someone does not want to speak and prefers to be silent, that is also very powerful."

In terms of transferability of this experience, while different learning and training programs would not be able to replicate the proseminar *per se*, a "professional seminar" could be created as a participant homeroom, in which learning to learn together is the focus, as opposed to learning about specific content. And if talking circles were not possible to enact, certainly facilitation methodologies that teach us how to engage with respect, in silence and voice, within a nonjudgmental environment are available to us all.

Practical Strategies for Learning to Learn Together

- Create structures that support, instead of hinder, adult learning and development.
- Utilize dialogue strategies that provide space for voice, silence, and listening.

- Support ways of learning together by common readings, shared experiences, and learner-initiated efforts.
- Understand that learning communities do not grow overnight and that compassion and patience, coupled with nurturing guidance, will help move a group of individuals to see their shared common goals.

THE FACULTY: FACILITATIVE LEADERS OF LEARNERS

Faculty and facilitators must be comfortable with the goal of building inclusive communities and guiding groups through discussions around difference. This says something about the selection, training, professional development, and evaluation of faculty and group facilitators, given the goals of the leadership and change doctoral program to use faculty who can successfully navigate the whitewater of social identities, their own and those of students. It also speaks to the ways in which faculty lead. Bell Hooks tells us to "employ pedagogical strategies that create ruptures in the established order, that promote modes of learning that challenge hegemony" (1994, p. 185). One of the ways we do this in the doctoral program is by requiring the sharing of experiences. There is an explicit focus on narratives, both as personal storytelling as well as a research methodology. This happens throughout the program in formal and informal ways, including specific written assignments, classroom sharing, and informal opportunities to bring one's whole self. Similarly, Boler and Zembylas outline a pedagogy of discomfort for understanding difference that emphasizes that students and faculty should be outside their comfort zones and "engage in critical inquiry that asks students to radically reevaluate their worldview" (2003, p. 111). Through readings and discussions, we encourage students to uncover their positionality, meaning reflecting on and understanding their own social identities and how those identities construct ways of knowing, not knowing, bias, and subjectivity and relating to the world around them, in virtually every assignment and to understand the standpoint of the scholars they read.

But as I've stated earlier, I focus less on the pedagogic content and curriculum strategies, and more on the relational work of faculty in order to allow positionality to surface and not implode. One student writes, "One of our faculty members introduced the notion of the leader as an instrument of change. I think that holds true for the faculty. I think their leadership influences the nature of the discussion." Certainly, Homan and Jehn, in their casebook chapter on organizational faultlines, remind us that transformational leadership behaviors can play a crucial role in improving negative group processes because of the information sharing and the degree to which individuals identify with the team. Faculty—when at their best—are transformational leaders who can facilitate transformational learning. As stated previously, in preparation for this chapter, I asked program faculty what they do that has the capacity to build positive relationships between individuals and that helps groups transcend individual social identities. A number of ideas were shared.

What comes to mind first are the important and basic behaviors that facilitate good discussion, as in the following list articulated by one faculty member:

- Try to listen carefully and be respectful of each other's humanity.
- Try not to make a quick judgment.
- Try to prevent dominant consensus from silencing numerical minority dissent (regardless of my own convictions).
- Model how to have discussions about "isms" without making it personal (no finger pointing; always relating individual to the larger societal levels and socio-political structures at play).
- Do corrective intervention when offensive things are being said without pushing the offender in a corner (preferably use humor rather than reprimanding, when appropriate).

Another faculty member approached the question by discussing the way in which she shifts away from traditional notions of faculty role and authority. "I spend a great deal of time," she writes, "attempting to provide an unconditional and safe space for the authentic voices of the students to emerge. Many of our students come from environments where the approach is 'stand and deliver.' There is a belief that an 'entertaining' professor who spills out lots of verbiage is the best. I prefer interactive teaching methods so that the primary teachers are the students themselves. I also prefer more silence from me so that I can truly 'hear' the voices of my students."

One of the more intangible facilitator capacities is the interpersonal skill that must be present in order to support this sort of safe environment. One faculty member writes, "I rely on my training as a therapist to create a safe learning environment in class, similar to trying to build rapport in a therapeutic situation. Being authentic, congruent, and accepting I think is paramount. A warm, supporting, and open atmosphere is necessary. Unconditional positive regard is also one of those big concepts that is very difficult to establish in a large or small group, especially if you deal with difficult concepts."

While faculty tended to focus on their strategies for facilitating good discussion or building rapport, as highlighted above, safety for students also came from surprising places. One student wrote that seeing faculty work together as a team when the unexpected occurred provided her with a sense of safety. In this particular example, two of our eight faculty could not attend a residency at the last minute because of family illnesses. As program director, I stood before the community and said, "This is what we will do. I'm not certain if it will work. What do you think?" Of that experience, the student writes, "In that moment, we were invited into the process. For me, when a leader is vulnerable and willing to show his or her vulnerability, it makes the space safer." Another writes, "The faculty never pretend to have all the answers, and that feels good."

The final comment offers an important lesson: to realize that learners feel safe when the "experts" don't pretend to know everything runs counter to the widely held belief that teachers are supposed to be all-knowing and "followers" feel safe when those in charge take full control. Clearly, the message we hear from adult learners is that they feel safe when they are brought into the change and when they have a voice in the process.

Practical Strategies for Facilitators and Faculty

- Follow best practices for facilitating dialogue, with special attention to leaving space for silence, ensuring that dominant voices don't overpower, and holding norms of respectful intellectual engagement.

- Hold all participants in positive regard and value their contributions.

- Don't pretend to know everything; allow for vulnerability. It apparently doesn't scare adult students at all.

FINAL THOUGHTS

In summary, my core feeling about how to create safe learning environments in which difference is addressed has little to do with techniques for dialogue, content of curriculum, or sophisticated methods of analysis. For me, it has most to do with creating a welcoming environment that tries to respect the whole person within the context of a mutually empowering purpose. It is as simple, and as complex, as that!

Using Film to Illustrate Different Perspectives

Clemson Turregano
Belinda B. McFeeters

When a truth on the screen collides with an individually held truth and reinforces or challenges our mental models, we feel challenged, warmed, and sometimes tearful. Many people cry at films because they relate to the characters. They see the truths they have lived and—through the film—they live their own stories.

Even though various theoretical perspectives suggest that people learn in many different ways, often facilitators and others who teach others fail to take this into account when trying to reach their audiences in the classroom and other venues. Instead, many only focus on standard, traditional teaching methods (Parker, Frye, & Robinson, 2006). As instructor facilitator, you may want to use film or another form of video media (YouTube or Facebook) to illustrate or make more "real" the experiences of difference illustrated in the cases.

Four primary modes of learning are discussed in Kolb's (1999) Learning Style Indicator inventory: learning through experience, reflection, theory, and experimentation. Facilitators can use film to engage learners in each of these modes because a full visual context is provided for the learner, thereby enhancing the learning experience.

Some of the questions you might be pondering may be: "What are some of the ways I can use film to enhance the learning experience for students? What are some of the planning considerations I need to take into account when I use movies in the classroom? What resources might I consider if I want to use film in the classroom? How can film help students explore situations in multiple perspectives?" This chapter seeks to address those questions, offering thoughts and suggestions on how you might help your students better understand differences through film.

Using film and guided discussions to teach is key for those who educate and train others (Champoux, 1999). This method provides many opportunities to advance student learning and improve pedagogy and presents a different perspective for students. Film offers insights to behavior, context, and a sensory understanding that is difficult to obtain from a textbook or lecture. When viewed during class, visual media offers the class a shared learning experience and the fuel for improved cohesion and collaboration. Even more important, visual media provides the framework for interaction following the viewing experience. When used improperly, however, films can reduce a sound theory to popular tidbits, distract the class with useless aphorisms, disorient the students with regard to the theory, and provide a poor substitute for actual engagement and interactive learning.

Film should be used to role model or illustrate differences, bringing in a different medium to demonstrate a different view of a theory or a topic. It demonstrates a broad and varied teaching approach and provides a diverse venue for student ideas and discussion other than simply texts, lectures, or examinations. Using film also enhances the learning value for visual learners, who will appreciate the change from the normal routine of the classroom.

In this chapter, we present some straightforward ideas about choosing and using movies in the classroom, and then address some frequently asked questions that we receive about using movies in the classroom. After reading this, you should feel more confident about the choice you have made to use movies in the classroom, your choice of instructional design, the choice of movie, and tying all of this to the learning objectives of your class.

SELECT FILMS FOR AND CONNECT FILMS TO THE LEARNING EXPERIENCE

To the extent possible, provide information that pushes participants to think more deeply or broadly about the core questions associated with the cases and to help participants make sense of the case using methods, frameworks, and theories that will help them in the "real world." The ability to reframe, for example, to explore a position from multiple perspectives, is a teaching method often used in organizational and management education (Bolman & Deal, 1984, 1991; Frost, Louis, Lundberg, & Martin, 1991; Morgan, 1986; Quinn, 1988). Instructors who want to incorporate examples of reframing in their classes often use film so that students can witness reframing in action (Gallos, 1993) and can imagine how these situations might apply in the real world.

One example of reframing takes place in *The Karate Kid,* a martial arts film with an underdog story line. Daniel, the underdog, meets a potential girlfriend and, during his pursuit of her, upsets her ex-boyfriend, a karate student. Because the ex-boyfriend and his friends now continuously pick fights and beat Daniel up, Daniel seeks karate training by Mr. Miyagi, a karate expert. Gallos (1993) notes that, through seemingly unconventional karate training practices, Mr. Miyagi demonstrates to Daniel how his household work (painting, deck sanding, and car waxing) is more than household duties, but are also key karate training techniques. Daniel is eventually able to reframe the days of hard work, which he refers to as "slave labor," to highly complex training preparation for a competitive karate championship.

When individuals have a good understanding of reframing, instructors might then explore the processes that influence reframing. The classic *Rashomon,* for example, involves four witnesses giving four different accounts of a rape and murder. This film allows individuals to see people framing the same event in strikingly different ways, based on their individual motives for telling the story the way they do. This discussion can lead to personal interpretations of what seemed to take place, tendencies to build individual theories, and shed light on the importance of multiple perspectives to fully understand what has taken place (Gallos, 1993).

Exploring the social implications of individual perspectives is also important when reframing. One film that does this well is *Dinner with Andre*. This film allows one to explore the depth of differences, possible reasons for those differences, and implications for a friendship. It takes an account of conversations between two men who have very different world views and beliefs about death, art, love, and the quest for self-fulfillment. It ultimately unveils the power and social consequences of contrasting ways of thinking (Gallos, 1993).

When it comes to eliminating resistance and stereotypes among diverse individuals, using film is another useful and non-threatening method to consider. Using the various perspectives found in different types of movies, developing awareness with students about how to manage differences and more effectively value diversity is supported (Parker, Frye, & Robinson, 2006). For example, in the movie *Pleasantville*, two 1990s teenagers are sent back into a 1950s sitcom. Filled with frequent metaphors, including a rose beginning to bloom and then turning red as one of the actors in the film has an eye-opening experience, the teen's encounters make up a very thought-provoking, technically amazing, and humanistic film that tells a real story about difference. With the film starting out in black and white, and shifting to color, it incorporates themes around diversity, individual change, cultural change, societal change, and community change. *Pleasantville's* use of color to show diversity, change, loss of identity, and a resistance to change makes it a very unique choice in film to use to study managing change and difference (Parker, Frye, & Robinson, 2006).

Although we've explored many examples of ways to use film effectively, using film to enhance the learning experience can sometimes be a double-edged sword. Although we want students and viewers to remember the purpose of the class, not just the excitement of the movie, students are somewhat conditioned to be passive when they watch films, when, as teachers, we want them to be exactly the opposite.

In addition, the film will be something the student may relate to more than the other material. Many times, students will remember the film and the fact it occurred in class much longer than they will remember the themes or points that the class was supposed to relate. Films, designed for entertainment, condition the student to relax and adapt a passive stance. Conditioned by their trips to the theater, they settle into the seats, kick back as it were, and get ready to let the movie flow over them. In some ways, this might be very helpful, for as the students are settling in for the film, they are also reducing the cognitive barriers to reality, allowing the mind to accept other ideas and principles.

Students then, with a willing acceptance to watch the film, are lowering their defense mechanisms to allow movies that are somewhat unrealistic to entertain and perhaps even enlighten them. It is in this space of suspended reality that the instructor must be most careful. If allowed to relax to a point of entertainment, the learning value is lost. However, if focused well by the instructor, students may still suspend their real judgment while being on the lookout for answers to the focus provided by the teacher. Often termed *purposeful viewing*, this directed observation provides the foundation for the film to support the teaching themes.

Purposeful viewing means to watch the film with a goal in mind. Give viewers an assignment to find examples, themes, or behaviors that translate to the topic being studied. Purposeful viewing can illuminate lessons for some types of learners that are not readily apparent through books, lecture, or even classroom interaction.

Films can reveal so many observable lessons that they have the opportunity to fast-forward a class in terms of the subject material. They have a way of taking very tough and complex ideas, and through an individual's interpretation of what is happening on the screen, they can begin to break down the complexity into more easily understood and digestible parts.

HOW TO ACHIEVE PURPOSEFUL VIEWING

Using purposeful viewing, participants can key into leadership behaviors that are both positive and negative. They can reflect on their own reactions to those behaviors and whether the behaviors are conducive to effective leadership in a context of difference. Purposeful viewing is not that hard to achieve. Prior to the film's start, either in the syllabus or in the class before the film, inform the students of the film and their reading requirements prior to its showing. Telling them that they will take an interactive part in watching the film enhances the interest in the film and may also get the students to actually do the reading. Tell them they will be assigned certain parts of the film to observe and then comment on during the discussion following the screening. Do not tell them what part they will be observing because you want them to do all the reading.

On the day of the class, when students enter the room, have the key question for learning on the board. Tell them a little about the background of the film and the main characters. This is very important, as students may have no personal reference to the context or perspectives shown. Also tell them what is happening when the film begins so they can be informed observers.

Viewing good films teaches us the real truth about how people think, act, and dream, therefore allowing us to gain a good understanding about what makes people tick. These are key factors when trying to understand different perspectives, are great skills to have as leaders, and are at the heart of purposeful viewing (Clemens & Wolf, 1999).

We keep these ideas in mind when I make the assignments. Because we teach leadership, we focus on people, relationships, behaviors, and outcomes. We might ask one group of students to focus on each topic, giving specific students a character to watch, tying the assignment into the learning for the day. Another student may observe the relationships between the characters—how they were formed, what sustained the relationships, or obstacles to relationships. A third group of students may observe key leadership behaviors that we may be studying, while a final group focuses purely on outcomes.

The idea of viewing with a purpose is the nexus of the educational experience and the entertainment. Depending on your questions, students are now fully engaged in accomplishing the objectives of the class while watching the film. Empowered as contributors, they are active observers, seeking to address the questions they have been assigned, knowing they will be asked to contribute to a discussion of their topic and how it interrelates with the others you have provided to the class.

Adopting purposeful viewing has many results. The discussion following the film is richer and focused on the learning objectives, not just the film, and helps students to understand how people see things differently. More than one student may be assigned a particular event or character to observe: however, each will have a different perspective. The depth of dialogue regarding the lesson's objectives is much more intense and broad. The movie gives participants a way to share their views in an easy manner, using vignettes from the film as examples. The themes of the class are thus anchored in the film, and the class discussion allows participants to use themes in the film to build deeper meaning of the lesson's objectives.

CONSIDERATIONS WHEN USING FILM

Cinema is a teaching enabler—it is not a substitute teacher. Many of us can remember a teacher turning on a film and telling us to take notes saying, "You will be tested." A travesty for education and for the film, this is not the way to use film. They are not substitutes, class fillers, compensation for poor planning, or a way to entertain students about the material. Films, like case studies, experiential activities, laboratories, or playing fields, are teaching tools that require forethought, planning, insight, application, and review.

There are a number of other things to consider when choosing films as teaching tools—the best films to use are those that are relevant to the topic, cinematically interesting, and theoretically revealing. First and foremost is relevance to the topic. This is the hardest aspect of identifying the correct film to pursue when teaching. Choose films that are relevant to the topic and portray the topic differently than a normal case study. Second, the film needs to be cinematically interesting. Keep in mind that what may be interesting to you may not be interesting to the students. So try to choose films that have favorable reviews for the intended audiences. In addition, ask for feedback about the films each time, and keep this information for future reference. Finally, a film needs to reveal the theoretical underpinnings of the topic in an insightful way that allows the students to grasp the importance of the topic.

Understanding film as a tool allows good educators to choose to use film as a tool to leverage the reading and themes of the class. Groups of readings prior to the film, with key topics listed, can serve as a sound foundation to leverage the film experience. A film with great relevance, that holds the students' interest, with a strong correlation to the material, can fast forward students' understanding and application of class themes long after the course has been completed.

FREQUENTLY ASKED QUESTIONS

Q: Should I show the whole film or just parts?

A: Like all answers, it depends. If you have time, show the entire film. Most instructors do not have two to three hours for a feature-length film, but try to show as much of the film as possible. In order to keep the class to three hours, you may use fifteen minutes for the opening and discussion, then start the film. This allows for a short break as well as about thirty minutes for the discussion following. If you are in a position to carry the discussion over to the next day, do so if necessary, but film details may not be as fresh in the minds of the participants if you wait longer than a day or so.

Another technique is to demonstrate behaviors from different films. If your class is focusing on a single topic, such as different interpretations of loyalty, you may want to show short clips from different films. Using purposeful viewing, each student keeps the same assignment, yet the films demonstrate different behaviors, offering the students the opportunity to compare and contrast their observations.

Q: Which is better—allowing students to watch the film on their own or watching it as a class?

A: When you watch the film as a class, you obtain an additional benefit from the film—a shared experience. Admittedly more difficult than just assigning a film to watch on their own, the shared experience may be a desired outcome. Like using an experiential activity conducted in a small group, the class now shares something in common that only they have. In addition, they can witness the reactions of other members in the class to the film and during the discussion following—providing an opportunity not only for deeper discussion, but also for further developing their reframing abilities, as well as forging intellectual bonds within the classroom around a topic.

This is not to say this cannot happen if a student watches the film on his or her. Given a good study guide and with the proper instructions for purposeful viewing, the student will usually take advantage of the time and watch the entire film, as opposed to just certain parts of the film. In addition, if the students watch the film outside the classroom, they have the time available to watch the additional material that often accompanies many of the DVDs today, including short vignettes regarding historical accuracy, different meanings in the film, and even greater depth about the characters in the film.

Q: What about copyrights?

A: The best bet is to consult the fair use principles of digital media with your organization's legal counsel. Generally, nonprofit institutions in the U.S. that use films for educational purposes in a classroom setting are typically approved. What is frowned upon is using films incorrectly—parts of films, films that have been illegally reproduced, and so forth. Again, the best answer is to discuss this with your organization's legal counsel.

OTHER SUGGESTED MOVIES AND DOCUMENTARIES FOR LEADERSHIP ACROSS DIFFERENCES

The list below contains key movies and documentary films that deal with diversity-related issues such as race, gender, sexual orientation, religion, and transformation.

Diversity and Change

- Ross, G. (1998). *Pleasantville*. Incorporates themes around diversity, individual change, cultural change, societal change, and community change. *Pleasantville* uses color to show diversity, change, loss of identity, and a resistance to change. Running time: 2 hours 3 minutes. Rated: PG-13.

Gender

- Biren, J. E. (2000). *Women organize!* An inspirational, half-hour video that portrays women organizers across the U.S. who are involved in the global struggles for racial, social, and economic justice. Running time: 32 minutes. Not rated.

- Caro, N. (2005). *North country*. Based on a true story relevant to the first class-action sexual harassment lawsuit in U.S. history. Running time: 126 minutes. Rated: R.
- Hadleigh-West, M. (1998). *War zone.* Powerful film about sexism and its implications. Record of day-to-day abuse that women experience in everyday life in four major cities. Running time: 98 minutes. Not rated.

Race and Ethnicity

- Haggis, P. (2004). *Crash*. Several stories interweave during two days in Los Angeles involving diverse characters from all walks of life dealing with various incidents around race, class, and justice. Running time: 112 minutes. Rated: R.
- Mun Wah, L. (1995). *The color of fear.* (Oakland, CA: Stir Fry Seminars). Racially diverse group spends a weekend together and dialogues about institutional and individual racism. Running time: 90 minutes. No rating noted.
- Ross, G. (1998). *Pleasantville*. Incorporates themes around diversity, individual change, cultural change, societal change, and community change. *Pleasantville* uses color to show diversity, change, loss of identity, and a resistance to change. Running time: 2 hours 3 minutes. Rated: PG-13.
- Singleton, J. (1995). *Higher learning*. People from various walks of life are faced with racial tension, responsibility, rape, and the meaning of getting a college education on a majority campus. Running time: 2 hours 7 min. Rated: R.

Racism and Sexism

- Butler, S. (1998). *The way home*. Shows affinity or caucus group dialoguing about racism, sexism, and related issues. Explores challenges of living in a white supremacist world. Running time: 92 minutes. Not rated.

Religion

- Kiley, R., (2003). *The gates of Jerusalem: A history of the holy city*. Documentary depicting the historical exploration of the Holy Land revealing Jerusalem's influence on religions around the world. Running time: 120 minutes. Not rated.

Sexual Orientation

- Chasnoff, D., & Cohen, H. (1996). *It's elementary: Talking about gay issues in school*. The opinions of first- through eighth-graders on homosexuality after discussing the topic with teachers in a nonjudgmental environment. Running time: 80 minutes. Not rated.

- Kaufman, M. (2000). *The Laramie project*. Based on the play by Moisés Kaufman and members of the Tectonic Theater Project about the reaction to the 1998 murder of University of Wyoming gay student Matthew Shepard in Laramie, Wyoming. The murder is widely considered to be a hate crime motivated by homophobia. Running time: 97 minutes. Not rated.

- Kushner, T. (2003). *Angels in America* (HBO mini-series). A political epic about the AIDS crisis during the mid-1980s, based around a group of separate but connected individuals. Running time: 352 min (6 parts). Not rated.

- Peirce, K. (1999). *Boys don't cry*. Thought-provoking and multi-layered filming of the infamous life and death of "Brandon Teena," who was a troubled woman who passed herself off as a man in rural Texas only to become the victim of a brutal hate crime. Running time: 118 minutes. Rated: R.

Socioeconomic Issues

- Cassavetes, N. (2002). *John Q*. A father and husband whose son is diagnosed with an enlarged heart finds out he cannot receive a transplant because HMO insurance will not cover it. He decides to take a hospital full of patients hostage until the hospital puts his son's name on the recipients' list. Running Time: 118 minutes. Rated: PG-13.

Transformation

- Kaye, T. (1998). *American History X*. Shows how a younger brother is influenced by his older brother's actions and ideology and how the older brother, now radically changed by his experience in confinement, tries to prevent his brother from going down the same path as he did. It deals with issues of transformation and racial identity development. Running time: 119 minutes. Rated: R.

- Washington, D. (2002). *Antwone Fisher*. A young navy man is forced to see a psychiatrist after a violent outburst against a fellow crewman. During the course of treatment, a painful past is revealed and a new hope begins. Running time: 120 minutes. Rated: PG-13.

Additional Resource

- Gerster, C., & Zlogar, L.W. (2006). Teaching ethnic diversity with film: Essays and resources for educators in history, social studies, literature, and film studies. Jefferson, NC: McFarland & Company.

Assessing Leadership Across Differences Sessions

Emily Hoole

Institutions are often accountable for assessing learning. However, a well-designed and implemented assessment process goes beyond meeting accountability requirements and helps instructors and participants understand and improve the learning experience. In this chapter, I provide information about how to develop and implement an assessment process that enhances your use of the materials in the casebook and this Facilitator's Guide, provides a systematic way to "check in" with participants, and that informs administrative decisions (such as assigning grades).

Before developing an assessment process, it is important to be clear about how you will use the data. There are a wide variety of potential uses; the ones that are most closely related to leadership across differences include:

- To inform decisions regarding whether participants are learning what you expect;
- To inform efforts to improve learning and development;
- To understand the progress of a group of participants;
- To determine whether instructional changes are necessary to achieve the goals of the program;

- To assign individual grades; and
- To determine the long-term effects of the program.

One helpful framework to consider is Kirkpatrick's (1994) four-level model of training evaluation. The model starts with gauging participant satisfaction and reaction to the session, along with the intent by the participant to apply what he or she has learned. The second level is learning gained as a result of the training or program, followed by transfer of learning to the real-world context. The final level is broader organizational impact. Evaluating or assessing all of these levels may be important to determining success. This chapter focuses primarily on the first level (participant satisfaction and intent to transfer) and on learning.

The uses listed above can be categorized as either data for improvement or data for decisions or judgment. Using data to diagnose learning preferences and needs, to measure aptitude, and/or to monitor progress are improvement-related uses. Data for decisions or judgments would be used to assign grades, rate performance, or measure instructional effectiveness. The focus of this chapter is on the assessment of learning rather than assessment of teaching. While there is clearly a relationship between teaching and learning, I do not focus on using assessment data to make judgments regarding the skill, effectiveness, or value of the facilitator (personnel evaluation is different from program evaluation).

Due to the sensitive nature of the topics associated with leadership across differences, it is critical to create a safe environment not only for instruction (as described in Alexandre's chapter), but for assessment as well. The challenge is to balance the need for psychological safety with the need to push students outside of their comfort zones for true learning and growth to occur and to understand the impact of learning. The information and activities in the *Leading Across Differences* materials are likely to challenge the ways participants think and believe, so it is important that the learning environment be supportive of exploration and not rife with unrealistic expectations or risks. Assessments should be developed and implemented in a way that provides safety to the respondents. Key to this is confidentiality of responses, direct constructive feedback, and opportunity for reflection.

OVERVIEW OF AN ASSESSMENT PROCESS

There are a number of steps in the development of an assessment process. In the following sections, I'll provide more detail about each step. But first, I'd like to provide an overview so you can see how the steps fit together.

First, clear objectives need to be written prior to the development of the instructional plan. The exercises described in this guide have recommended objectives associated with them, but depending on how you use or combine the exercises, you may want to write your own objectives. Once you know the objectives you want to achieve, you can plan your instruction. Be sure that the objectives you seek and instructional design you plan to use are tightly coupled. The objectives can be thought of as the intended outcomes, whereas the assessment data you collect later are the actual outcomes (Erwin, 1991). Next, decide how the objectives will be measured. Various methods can be employed to measure progress toward an objective. Considering the pros and cons of each method and examining issues of reliability and validity is necessary. Finally, the assessment is carried out and the results utilized by the instructor and participants to understand the process and outcomes of the learning experience. These results may be used to improve the learning experience or to help substantiate that the participants are achieving the expected outcomes. In the following paragraphs, I address each of the steps indicated above.

Step 1. Write Objectives

Writing objectives, along with selecting the appropriate assessment method(s), is often the most challenging aspect of assessing learning and development, especially for courses that are focused on something as complex and nuanced as leadership across differences. Good objectives are hard to write, and during the process of writing objectives you may change your thinking regarding the session or course. Learning objectives may be knowledge-based or developmental in nature. Knowledge-based objectives relate to the subject matter and content of the material. Developmental objectives are of three types: higher-level cognitive processing, affective, and, conative (Shavelson, Roeser, Kupermintz, Lau, Ayala, Haydel, Schultz, Gallagher, & Quihuis, 2002). A good framework for developing cognitive objectives is Bloom's Taxonomy (Bloom & Krathwohl, 1956) (see Table 4). Utilizing this framework along with the action verbs associated with each level of the taxonomy can assist in the process of writing these types of objectives.

In addition to knowledge, skill-based, and cognitive objectives, programs utilizing the LAD casebook may have developmental objectives that are affective or conative in nature. Affective objectives are related to emotions, feelings, and beliefs. In this context, they may relate to changes in perspectives, development of more positive feelings regarding other social identity groups, or fundamental changes in world view. Conation combines motivation and volition and deals with constructs such as confidence, investment of effort/persistence, and bias toward action. Writing (and measuring) developmental objectives can be even more difficult than knowledge-based objectives. Gable's (1986) categories of affective characteristics (see Table 5) provide a good basis on which to draft objectives.

Table 4. Bloom's Taxonomy and Sample Learning Objectives

Bloom's Taxonomy	Sample Learning Objectives
	Participants will be able to . . .
Knowledge: *Define, identify, label, state, list, match*	Match examples of triggers to the type of trigger represented.
Comprehension: *Describe, generalize, paraphrase, summarize, estimate*	Identify and describe the social identity issue that exists in the trigger event.
Application: *Determine, chart, implement, prepare, solve, use, develop*	Construct a case (real or imagined) that includes all of the relevant components of a social identity conflict (multiple groups, trigger event, spillover).
Analysis: *Point out, differentiate, distinguish, discriminate, compare*	Compare and contrast a conflict situation from the multiple social identity perspectives present.
Synthesis: *Create, design, plan, organize, generate, write*	Develop a plan of action for a conflict situation using the Leadership Across Differences Framework.
Evaluation: *Appraise, critique, judge, weigh, evaluate, select*	Review a situation and plan of action and provide feedback regarding the potential effectiveness of the intervention.

While there is no recognized and established taxonomy of conative objectives, following are some examples. Participants will

- Increase their self-confidence in dealing with social identity conflicts in the workplace.
- Be motivated as managers/leaders to address conflicts involving social identity issues in the workplace.

- Act in an ethical manner when faced with a complex social identity issue.
- Utilize a variety of flexible strategies to resolve a social identify conflict.

Table 5. Gable's Categories of Affective Characteristics

Category	Example Affective Objectives
	Participants will . . .
Self-concept: *Feelings about one's self*	Develop a more positive self-image if they are from a minority social identity group.
Attitudes: *Feelings toward other people, ideas, institutions*	Recognize and articulate their own social identity biases when reviewing a conflict situation.
Interests: *Preferences regarding activities and areas of interest (e.g., sports, arts, travel, culture, technology)*	Develop greater interest in learning about different cultures by increasing interaction with different social identity groups in the workplace or community.
Values: *Ideas and beliefs that shape ways of life*	Develop and display greater empathy for all the parties engaged in a social identity conflict in the workplace or community.

Learning objectives are used in making decisions regarding improvement and judging the success of the effort. An assessment-for-improvement question would focus on the level of progress participants are making on objectives during the course of instruction to determine whether additional instruction or class focus is necessary to achieve the primary goals of the course. Objectives are used to make judgments when grades are assigned based on overall achievement or to determine the success of the course based on the overall growth and development of the participants.

Step 2. Decide How Objectives Will Be Measured

There are three primary methods used in assessments: (1) selected-response, which requires the responder to select a response from predetermined options, for example, multiple-choice and matching; (2) constructed response, which requires responders to create their own responses, such as an essay, project, or portfolio; and (3) behavioral assessment, which requires either self-report of daily behavior within context, observation, or multi-rater feedback. Table 6 presents the pros and cons and common uses for each of the three methods.

Table 6.
Assessment Methods

Method	Selected Response	Constructed Response	Behavioral
Pros	Easier to score and calculate reliability and validity statistics.	Less time to develop items and rubrics compared to selected-response items.	Helps to establish whether the program led to changes in behavior related to social identity conflicts.
Cons	More challenging to measure higher level of Bloom's taxonomy. Cannot effectively measure behavior.	Harder to establish reliability and validity of the data.	Significant development time required to create an assessment that yields reliable and valid data.
Common Uses	Use to measure knowledge-based objectives, self-reported attitudes, and beliefs at the end of the program. Can be used for pre- and post-test.	Use to measure higher levels of Bloom's taxonomy (analysis, synthesis, evaluation) and to uncover changes in values and beliefs as a result of the program.	Use to determine whether changes in knowledge and beliefs led to actual behavior change.

For many learning objectives, it will be important to compare data from several assessments—a process called triangulation. There are many ways to triangulate information. *Multiple sessions* can be assessed to investigate the process of instruction or substantiate the overall impact of the class. *Multiple methods* can be used to assess outcomes using both multiple-choice and constructed-response measures during the program, at the end of the program, or post-program.

Multiple perspectives can be gathered to verify behavior changes as a result of the program. And finally, including *multiple individuals* in the interpretation of the assessment data can help to validate findings and recommendations that are made based on the data.

Step 3. Determine the Quality and Appropriateness of the Assessments

The concepts of reliability, validity, and bias are critical to take into account when designing and developing assessments. Reliability is the degree to which an assessment produces consistent results. Think of a scale you have at home. If you get on the scale five times in a row and get a different weight each time, the data are not reliable and would indicate that something is wrong with the measure, a scale in this case. Validity is the combination of two ideas: (1) the degree to which an assessment measures what it claims to measure and (2) the usefulness of assessment data for a given purpose. Using the scale example again, your home scale may give you the same weight each time you step on it, but when you go to the doctor's office and step on his or her recently calibrated scale, your weight is different. So your scale at home provides you with reliable (consistent) data, but that data is not a valid representation of your weight and should not be used for judging whether your efforts to lose weight have been successful. In the same way, an assessment may not measure the objective you have written, and using the data to make inferences regarding changes in knowledge, motivation, and behavior may be incorrect. For additional resources, visit www.ncme.org/pubs/items/ITEMS_Mod_3.pdf.

A final concern is bias. Bias occurs when participants of different groups (gender, race, ethnicity, social identity group) are either disadvantaged or advantaged in responding to certain items or assessment approaches, leading to skewed responses. When developing an assessment, instructors should be aware of their own social identity biases and work to eliminate them from the assessment. Having colleagues from other social identity groups review the assessment may also help to identify and eliminate any obvious biases.

Step 4. Implement Assessment

After the objectives are written and the assessment methods aligned with the objectives, the assessment process is implemented. First you must decide when to assess. Here are some ways in which you might implement an assessment process:

- Assess participants prior to an LAD session to determine their level of knowledge or current beliefs or perceptions prior to being exposed to the material and the experience. This data can be used to help you target your facilitation and/or could be used later for a pre/post comparison.
- Assess participants during the middle of instruction to determine whether participants are getting the content and concepts or whether a mid-course correction is needed. This might be an informal process of asking for feedback from the group verbally or a quick written/electronic response to some questions that you can review during a break.
- Assessment directly after facilitation of the content can help determine whether participants had a favorable reaction or intend to apply what they learned.
- Assessment at the end of the entire course or program can help determine participants' level of achievement or provide evidence of growth or development.

Some key points to keep in mind when implementing the assessment process: (1) make sure participants are clear regarding the objectives of the session and understand how they will be assessed; (2) provide clear instructions for each assessment and each item so participants understand the task; (3) provide sufficient time to complete the assessment—this may range from an hour to complete a multiple-choice assessment to several weeks or months to complete a project; and (4) make sure sufficient time has passed for participants to have achieved the objective. If behavior is to be assessed after the program, make sure participants have had enough time to develop and demonstrate the new or different behavior targeted by the program before assessing.

Assessment can serve as an additional learning experience for participants if they are engaged in the process and allowed time for reflection. Deliberately calling participants' attention to the process of assessment before, during, and after the session as a way for them to evaluate their own personal progress and learning in order to set goals for the future can be a powerful experience.

Step 5. Interpret Data

Since a variety of important decisions may be made based on the interpretation of the data, there are a number of steps and issues to take into account. As mentioned earlier, it is important to engage multiple perspectives in the interpretation of the data. Solicit participants' or colleagues' feedback regarding the results and probe more deeply into whether the data you have collected accurately reflects the participants' experience and learning. Participants may be able to tell you that they have changed in significant ways that aren't reflected in the assessment results. Or they may provide strong agreement that the results do represent the program's impact.

Be sure to conduct an appropriate level of analysis. If you gathered data prior to a session and re-administered the same assessment after a session, compare the data to see whether participants have changed or increased knowledge and ability. If you are gathering the same data over time or with different groups concurrently, analyze and interpret the data to determine whether results are consistent or whether there are differences between groups based on changes to content or facilitation. Focus on interpreting the data in alignment with the objectives. Is there sufficient evidence to determine whether objectives were achieved to an acceptable level? If 25 percent of participants experience a significant shift in their perspectives regarding social identity conflicts, is that an acceptable result, or is the target 75 percent? Ninety percent?

Examine the data for unintended consequences (the objectives are your intended consequences)—both positive and negative. Do the data indicate that participants learned or gained something from the session that you didn't expect? Do they envision applying what they learned in a novel way you didn't think of? Did the session cause an unfavorable shift in perspective or cause some participants to feel threatened or attacked? Be sure to be on the lookout for these unintended consequences and take them into account when revising the program.

Step 6. Use Assessment Data

Using assessment data should not be a one-time occurrence at the conclusion of a session or program. For assessment to be most effective, especially for improvement purposes, ongoing interpretation and utilization are necessary. Don't wait to react when assessment data indicates changes need to be made to better meet participants' needs or the goals of the session.

Based on your own and others' interpretation of the data, decide what changes can be made in order to improve the session. Decide how you might test out different approaches in the future to determine what is most effective in helping participants achieve the objectives. If the data indicate the effort was successful, be sure to communicate that result to key stakeholders.

Be aware of some important ethics in using assessment data. Be sure to accurately report the results, both good and bad. People become suspicious when only good results are reported. For the data to be used most effectively, reporting negative findings can help spur necessary changes. List the limitations to the data or the analysis. This helps others to determine whether the assessment procedures were sound and how much confidence should be placed on the interpretations of the results. Make sure to observe the privacy and confidentiality of the participants' data. And finally, continue to check for bias—in the assessment, in the interpretation, and in recommendations made as a result of the assessment.

CONCLUSION

Assessment of learning and development is a critical component to any effective course of instruction, and the steps outlined above can lead to the development of an ongoing cycle of learning and improvement. Assessment within the context of leadership across differences has some unique challenges, given the nature of the content, but it is possible to implement an effective assessment process with some consideration and planning.

PART THREE
Individual Exercises

The following exercises are designed to help participants apply the knowledge in the LAD casebook to the situations in the cases and, more importantly, to their situations. All of these exercises appear in the casebook (with some minor modifications) and are intended to be used by one person. However, in the following section there are exercises designed specifically for pairs and small groups. Note that chapters referred to within the exercises are in the casebook, not in this Facilitator's Guide.

Mapping Your Social Identities

exercise
ONE

Objective: This exercise gives you an opportunity to explore your social identity by creating a social identity map and reflecting on it. You will also explore how your social identity might influence your ability to lead effectively in organizations.

Key concepts: social identity, given identity, chosen identity, core identity, leadership, multiple identities, simultaneity of identities identity mapping, life roles.

Relevant cases: all cases

Relevant Chapters
- Chapter 1: Social Identity: Understanding the In-Group/Out-Group Phenomenon
- Chapter 4: Leadership Practices Across Social Identity Groups

Time required: Approximately 60 minutes.

Learning Outcomes

1. Articulate one's given identity, chosen identity, and core identity.
2. Identify the influence social identity has on others and the leadership implications.

Materials
- Blank identity map
- Pen/pencil

When to use: At any time in a session.

Physical setting: A room in which participants can comfortably be seated at tables and view their identity maps.

EXPLANATION OF TERMINOLOGY: COMPONENTS OF IDENTITY

Your identity is a combination of three broad components: given identity, chosen identity, and core identity. Each of these components is described below.

Given identity. The attributes or conditions that you have no choice about are your given identity. They may be characteristics you were born with, or they may have been given to you in childhood or later in life. Elements of your given identity include birthplace, age, gender, birth order, physical characteristics, certain family roles, and possibly religion.

Chosen identity. These are the characteristics that you choose. They may describe your status as well as attributes and skills. Your occupation, hobbies, political affiliation, place of residence, family roles, and religion may all be chosen.

Core identity. These are the attributes that you think make you unique as an individual. Some will change over the course of your lifetime; others may remain constant. Elements of your core identity may include traits, behaviors, beliefs, values, and skills.

Some attributes may overlap or appear in two categories. Different people could put the same aspect of their identities in different categories depending on how much of a choice it felt like to them. For instance, your religious affiliation could be seen as either a given or a chosen aspect of your identity.

Many attributes are also subjective. One person's interpretation of "educated" may not match another's definition. Others may assume that you have chosen certain characteristics when, from your vantage point, you had little or no choice. Perhaps you were expected to go into the family business and never really made a choice about your profession.

Finally, context matters. Parts of your identity that matter to you may not matter to others, or may matter only in certain situations. Aspects of your identity that seem insignificant to you could become huge benefits or obstacles when you are working in certain situations or with particular groups. In your own country, you may leverage local culture to build rapport with others, but when traveling to other countries, you may downplay your culture and leverage your education and career credentials.

INSTRUCTIONS

Creating a map of your identity is a way to capture and articulate how you see yourself. You can begin with surface-level identities and then dig deeper. This can be useful in exploring how others may perceive you as a leader—who will feel more comfortable with you, who will give your words more weight, and so on. Your identity map should include the three components discussed in the previous section: given identity, chosen identity, and core identity.

Look at the sample map on the next page.

Using the blank map provided later in this exercise, follow these instructions to map your own identity.

1. In the outer ring, write words that describe your given identity, the attributes or conditions that you had no choice about, from birth or later. You may want to include your nationality, age, gender, physical characteristics, certain family roles, possibly religion. Examples include female, only child, forty-eight, tall, blind, African-American, cancer patient, widow.

2. In the next ring, list aspects of your chosen identity. Consider including your occupation, hobbies, political affiliation, where you live, certain family roles, possibly religion. Examples are cyclist, mother, engineer, expatriate, college graduate, wife, leader, New Yorker, Buddhist.

3. In the center, write your core attributes—traits, behaviors, beliefs, values, and skills that you think make you unique as an individual. Select things that are relatively enduring about you or that are key to who you are today. For example, you may see yourself as funny, artistic, kind, conservative, attentive, creative, impatient, musical, family focused, assertive.

Sample Identity Map

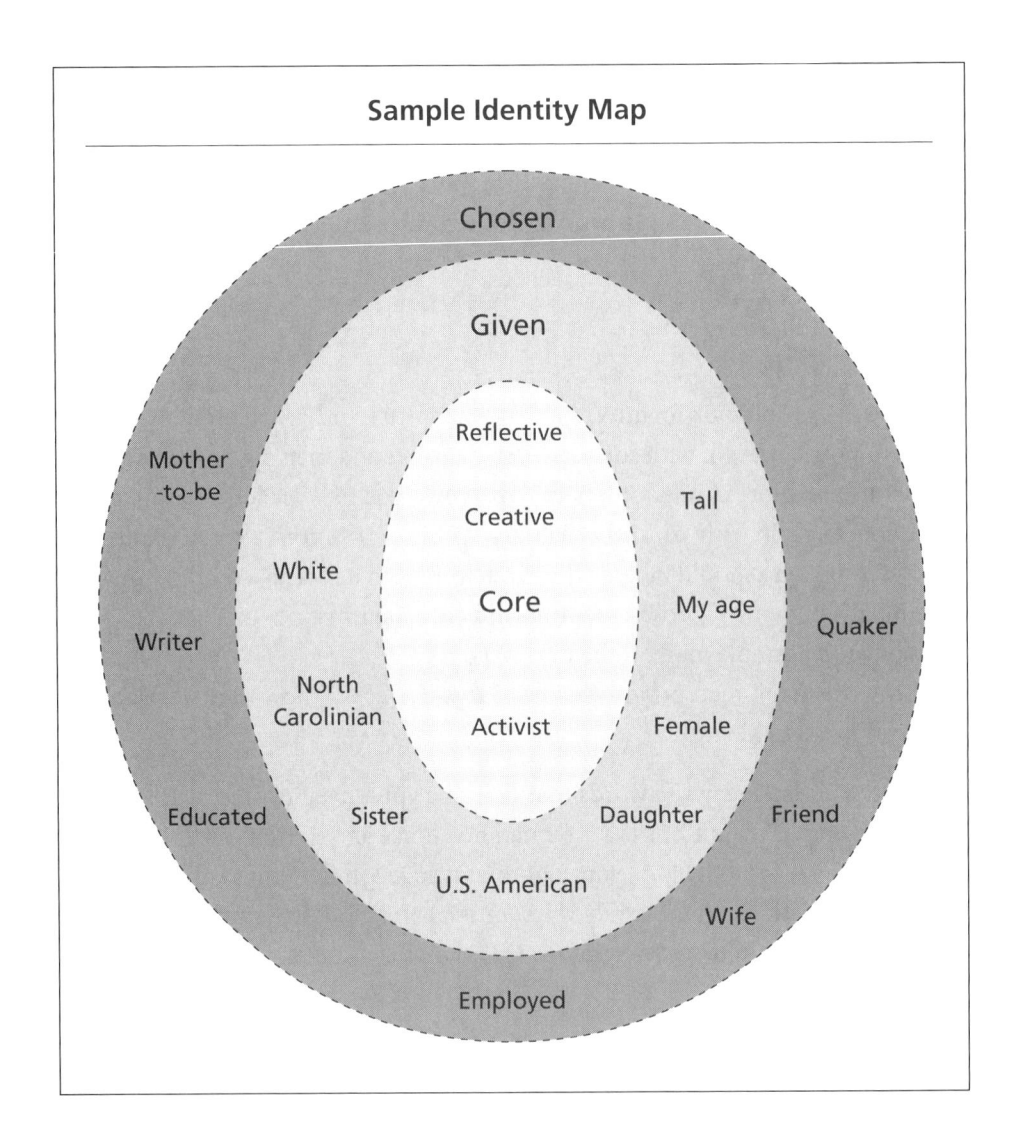

- Chosen
  - Mother-to-be
  - Writer
  - Educated
  - Friend
  - Quaker
  - Wife
  - Employed
- Given
  - White
  - Tall
  - North Carolinian
  - My age
  - Sister
  - Female
  - Daughter
  - U.S. American
- Core
  - Reflective
  - Creative
  - Activist

4. After you complete your map:
   - Underline the items that are important to you personally. These are likely to be the terms you would use to describe yourself.
   - Put a plus sign (+) beside the items that you believe contribute to your ability to lead effectively in your organization.
   - Put a minus sign (−) beside the items that you believe detract from your ability to lead effectively in your organization.
   - Put a question mark (?) beside the items that may vary in how they affect your leadership ability, depending on context.

Blank Identity Map

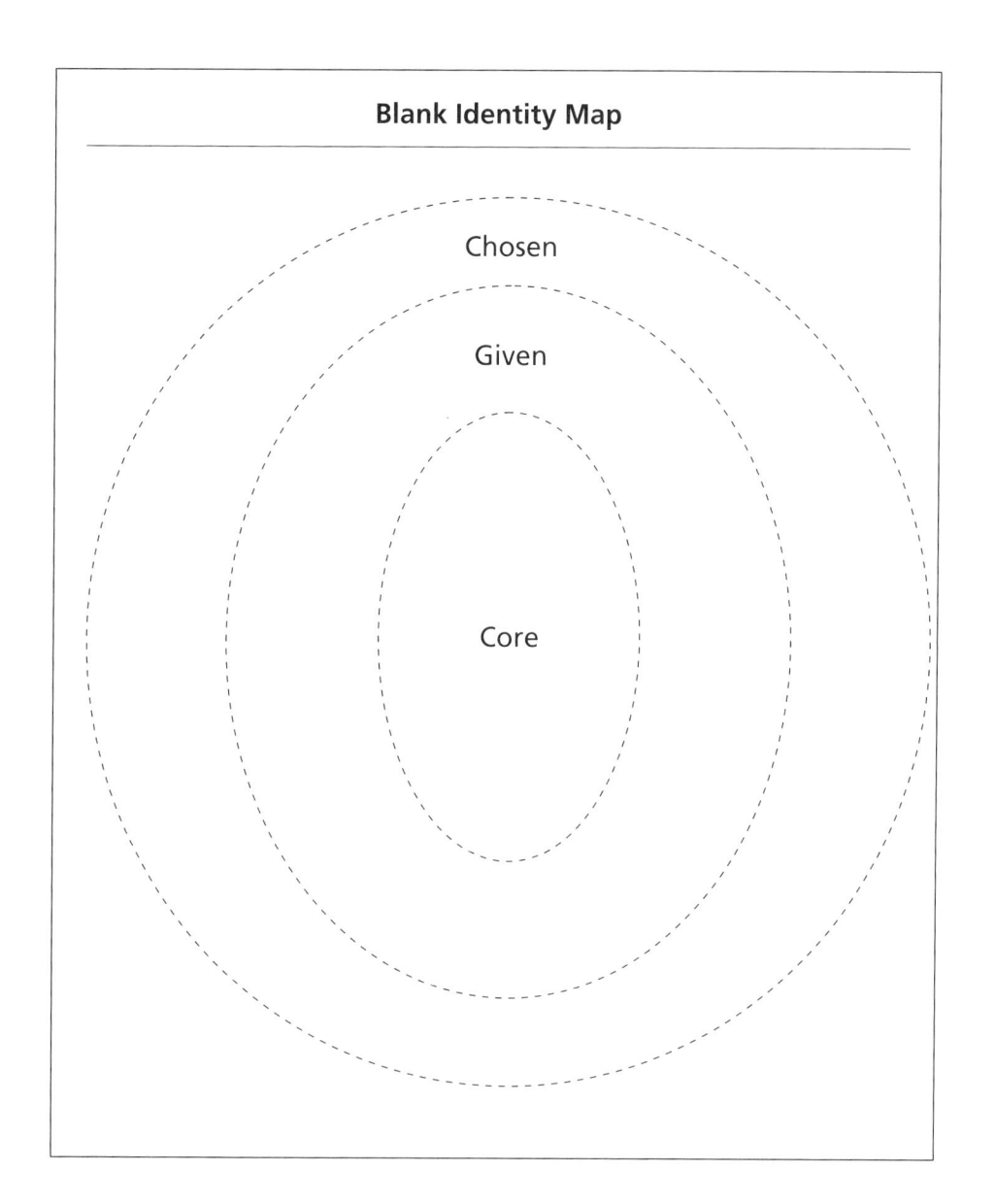

Chosen

Given

Core

Mapping Your Social Identities

INTERPRETING YOUR MAP

Refer to your map while answering the following questions. They will help you examine your social identity in more depth.

1. When you look at the underlined items on your map, what trends do you see? Are they mainly part of your given, chosen, or core identity?

   _____
   _____
   _____
   _____

2. When you look at the items with pluses, minuses, and question marks, what trends do you see? Are they mainly part of your given, chosen, or core identity?

   _____
   _____
   _____
   _____

3. Of the aspects with pluses, minuses, and question marks, which are things you have in common with other people in the organization? Which are things that only you or a very small number of people possess? What are the leadership implications?

   _____
   _____
   _____
   _____

4. What aspects of your identity help you make connections with people at work? What aspects of your identity get in the way of making connections with people at work? What gives you the impression that this is the case?

5. Are there aspects of your identity that you keep hidden at work? What impact might that have on you and those around you?

6. How might you reveal or emphasize particular elements of your identity at work in order to build or improve relationships?

7. How might you hide or deemphasize particular elements of your identity at work in order to build or improve relationships?

UNDERSTANDING OTHER IDENTITY PERSPECTIVES

People make assumptions about their social identities and those of others. When it comes to working with others, assumptions are often treated as reality. Assumptions can influence a person's beliefs about other people's thoughts and their motives for behaving the way they do.

Use the following questions to think through some of these assumptions. It may help to keep a particular person in mind when answering the questions (someone you've just met, someone you have problems with, etc.).

1. When you are building a relationship at work, what do you want to know about the other person? What do you notice first? Are you attracted to certain characteristics in others?

   _____
   _____
   _____
   _____

2. What assumptions do you make about other people based on their social identities?

   _____
   _____
   _____
   _____

3. If someone else were mapping your identity, what do you think he or she would notice first? What would be most relevant to him or her? Why?

_____

_____

_____

_____

4. What assumptions do you think other people make about you based on your social identity?

_____

_____

_____

_____

5. If you were to see the identity maps of other people with whom you work, how much do you think you would have in common with them?

_____

_____

_____

_____

6. What are the areas that would probably be different?

_____

_____

_____

_____

Your Experience with Triggers

exercise
TWO

Objective: This exercise prompts you to reflect on situations that may have triggered social identity conflicts and think about how these events align with social and power conflicts in general. This exercise encourages you to examine the role your values may have played in your experience with conflict, potentially revealing your "hot buttons" when it comes to triggers.

Key concepts: social identity and power conflict, triggers/trigger events differential treatment, assimilation, insults/humiliating acts, different values, simple contact

Relevant cases: all cases

Relevant Chapters
- Chapter 2: Triggers of Social Identity Conflict
- Chapter 3: Organizational Faultlines

Time required: Approximately 20 minutes

Learning Outcomes

1. Identify and understand how one's experiences with triggering events align with social and power conflicts in society at large.
2. List solutions that an individual or an organization can implement to prevent faultline activation and conflict in the future.

Materials

- Pen/pencil

When to use: In the middle or toward the end of a session following activities on social identity conflict or in a session that helps identify general diversity information.

Physical setting: A room in which participants can comfortably be seated at tables and view their trigger tables, and large enough to walk around and talk to each other.

INSTRUCTIONS

Understanding and identifying triggers is a foundational skill needed to lead across differences. Because social identity conflicts are generally emotional in nature and often reflect social and power relationship in society at large, the ability to recognize triggering events and their connections with societal issues is key.

Step 1: Identifying Triggers

Review the trigger descriptions in the table below and think about situations in which you have experienced events that may have triggered social identity conflicts. Choose one or more of the triggers that you have the most experience with and jot down a few notes about each experience as it pertains to the triggers listed below. In this step, focus on describing the situation: Who was involved? What happened? Where did the situation occur? (You'll complete the Social/Power Issues column in Step 2.)

Trigger	Description	Your Experience	Social/Power Issues
Differential Treatment	Occurs when one group perceives that another group has an advantage when it comes to the allocation of resources, rewards, opportunities, or punishments		

Assimilation	Occurs when the majority group expects that others will act just like them; there is an expectation that non-dominant groups will blend into the dominant culture		
Insults or Humiliating Acts	Occurs when a comment or behavior devalues or offends one group relative to another		
Different Values	Occurs when groups have decidedly different values; a clash of fundamental beliefs regarding what is wrong and what is right		
Simple Contact	Occurs when anxiety and tension between groups is high in the broader society; simple contact between these groups triggers a faultline		

Step 2: Interpreting Triggers

Interpret how these triggering events are connected with social and power conflicts in society at large and how you interpret the situation. Complete the Social/Power Issues column in the previous table. See the example for the Differential Treatment trigger below.

Trigger	Trigger Description	Your Experience	Social/Power Issues
Example: *Differential Treatment*	Occurs when one group perceives that another group has an advantage when it comes to the allocation of resources, rewards, opportunities, or punishments (this example is based on Case 3)	I wanted to be able to take a paid holiday on a day important in my religion rather than have a paid holiday associated with another religion.	The idea that the "majority rules" can reinforce policies and norms that further marginalize groups not in the majority. I feel that those in the majority don't realize or appreciate the advantage of having rules and policies that favor them. I don't understand why it has to be such a struggle for me to get what others take for granted.

Step 3: Reflection: Identifying Patterns, Gathering Perspectives, and Developing Ideas for Action

Being sensitive to triggers enables individuals and organizations to address issues, ideally preventing issues from deepening the divide between groups.

To assess your organization's propensity to effectively respond to triggering events, as well as your own, answer the questions below:

1. Are there certain triggers with which you have numerous or particularly painful experience? If so, what impact might that have on your ability to see other perspectives regarding similar situations?

___

___

2. How do you express your perspective with someone very different from you without trying to convince the person that your way is the "right" way?

3. How comfortable are you listening to a perspective that is very different from your own? How do you tend to react when you feel your values are challenged or threatened?

4. What actions have you or your organization taken to gain a deeper understanding of the different perspectives related to social identity issues within the organization?

5. Do certain kinds of triggers seem to happen more often within the organization? If so, what contributes to their occurrence?

6. What are some of the things you or your organization can do to gain a deeper understanding of the potential triggers within the organization?

IDEA FOR FURTHER EXPLORATION

Ask someone about his or her experiences with triggers and how he or she felt as a result. Listen without judging or questioning the person's perspective—just listen to the story and thank the person for sharing it.

Identifying Faultlines

exercise
THREE

Objective: This exercise is designed to help you identify potential faultlines in your work groups or other teams.

Key concepts: faultlines
Relevant cases: 5, 6, 8, 9, 10, 11, 12, 13

Relevant Chapters
- Chapter 3: Organizational Faultlines
- Chapter 4: Leadership Practices Across Social Identity Groups

Time required: Approximately 30 minutes

Learning Outcome

1. Identify potential faultlines in groups or teams.

Materials
- Pen/pencil

When to use: At any time during a session.
Physical setting: A room in which participants can comfortably be seated at tables and do reflection.

INSTRUCTIONS
Step 1
Think about a team or a group to which you currently belong or you belonged to in the past. Ideally, the team or group is work-related, but if needed you can

think of a group or team from another aspect of your life. Recall the members of the team and the nature of the work you were doing together.

Step 2

Using the rating scale below, rate the extent to which the team or group was different along the following dimensions. There are several blank lines on which you can insert additional dimensions if appropriate.

To what extent is the team or group similar in terms of . . .	Very Little Difference	⟵⟶		A Lot of Difference
Race				
Gender				
Religion				
Nationality				
Language spoken				
Educational level				
Age				
Functional background				

Of the differences in the team/group, did (or do) any of the differences co-occur, such that members are different in terms of more than one characteristic and subgroups are similar in terms of more than one characteristic? If so, which characteristics co-occur?

_____

_____

_____

_____

Research suggests that groups that are very similar and groups that contain a lot of differences are less likely to experience faultlines, because similar groups do not have many differences and groups with a great deal of difference have so many differences that subgroups tend not to form. However, it is also interesting to note that the salience and prominence of the differences influences the degree to which faultlines may be experienced.

Step 3

1. Next, think about the context in which the group or team was (or is working). How clear was the task on which the team was working?

   _____
   _____

2. How clear were the roles of various group or team members?

   _____
   _____

3. What practices (see the Leadership Practices Across Social Identity Groups chapter) were used in the team and how effective were they?

   _____
   _____
   _____

4. Can you think of ways to improve your diverse interactions with work team or group members in the future? What about your work groups and teams as a whole?

   _____
   _____
   _____

Cultural Values

exercise **FOUR**

Objective: This exercise is designed to help you think about decisions or choices you've made that may have had an effect on a colleague, group, or organization. You are encouraged to reflect on your preferred cultural values and the roles those values typically play in your own decision making and in that of others.

Key concepts: cultural values, decision making, autonomy vs. embeddedness, egalitarianism vs. hierarchy, harmony vs. mastery

Relevant cases: 2 through 13

Relevant Chapters
- Chapter 5: Cultural Values
- Chapter 10: Leader Values and Authenticity

Time required: Approximately 20 to 30 minutes

Learning Outcomes
1. Articulate the role one's preferred cultural values play in decision making and how values impact others.
2. Recognize how cultural value orientations impact decision making.

Materials
- Pen/pencil

When to use: At any time in a session.

Physical setting: A room in which participants can comfortably be seated at tables and do reflection.

INSTRUCTIONS

First, review the Cultural Values chapter in the casebook with the descriptions of the different value orientations. Think about decisions or choices you've made that may have had an effect on a colleague, group, or organization. List those decisions/choices in the first column below. Next, list your cultural value(s)—practices, symbols, specific norms, personal values—that influenced the decision or choice you made. Third, describe how your decision affected your colleagues, group, or organization. How did they react to your decision? Last, determine which value orientation is most closely related to the decision you made based on your cultural values, and circle the end of the orientation you prefer in the last column.

Cultural Values Assessment

Decision or choice I've made that may have had an effect (positive or negative) on a colleague or organization.	Cultural values that influenced my decision and how (personal values, norms, beliefs, symbols, practices)	How my decision affected my colleague, group, or organization	Value orientation used (circle the end of the value orientation you prefer):
Decision 1			Autonomy vs. Embeddedness
			Egalitarianism vs. Hierarchy
			Harmony vs. Mastery

Decision 2			Autonomy vs. Embeddedness
			Egalitarianism vs. Hierarchy
			Harmony vs. Mastery
Decision 3			Autonomy vs. Embeddedness
			Egalitarianism vs. Hierarchy
			Harmony vs. Mastery
Decision 4			Autonomy vs. Embeddedness
			Egalitarianism vs. Hierarchy
			Harmony vs. Mastery

SELF-EXAMINATION AND REFLECTION

1. "Leaders who recognize and take account of the cultural value orientations that influence their beliefs and actions and those of the people with whom they work are more likely to successfully lead in contexts of difference." Which are your preferred cultural values and what role do those values typically play in your own decision making?

   _____

   _____

   _____

   _____

2. How does understanding the role your cultural values play in your decision making affect your leadership style?

   _____

   _____

   _____

   _____

3. How did learning about the cultural value orientations impact your thinking about diverse perspectives and different ways of leading?

   _____

   _____

   _____

   _____

Approaches to Difference

exercise **FIVE**

Objective: The purpose of this exercise is to introduce two new orientations/perspectives that will help you understand your orientation to differences and describe working relationships with others outside of your social identity groups.

Key concepts: xenophobia, allophilia, social identity, in-group and out-group behavior, dual identities, recategorizing, decategorizing.

Relevant cases: 6, 9, 11, 13

Relevant Chapter
- Chapter 6: Approaches to Difference: Allophilia and Xenophobia

Time required: Approximately 30 minutes

Learning Outcomes
1. Define xenophobia and allophilia.
2. Identify one's orientation to social identity differences.
3. Develop ways to improve future encounters with individuals from different social identity groups.

Materials
- Magazines or Internet access, from which an image can be selected
- Pen/pencil

When to use: In the middle or toward the end of a session following activities on social identity conflict or in sessions that help identify workplace diversity

Physical Setting: A room large enough for participants to work on large tables or the floor to page through the magazines.

INSTRUCTIONS

Step 1: Identifying an Image

Read the Approaches to Difference chapter. Then leaf through images (in magazines or online) and identify a picture that represents how you feel when you encounter someone very different from you, in general.

For example, take a look at the figure of puzzle pieces below. This image could represent an individual's sense that others he or she encounters have more perspectives to consider (and thus more puzzle pieces), and enable a person to see a bigger picture, which creates feelings of excitement and fulfillment. However, the same image could represent an individual's sense that things are coming apart or are more divided—making it difficult to know what fits together and creating feelings of anxiety and perhaps resentment.

Picture of Puzzle Pieces

Step 2: Interpreting the Image

Looking at the image you selected and thinking about what it represents in terms of how you approach differences, answer the following questions:

1. What expectations do you have about the encounter?

___

2. What feelings tend to surface for you about the situation? Is it something positive? Uncomfortable, but necessary? Or something you'd rather avoid if possible?

___

3. In general, are you someone who actively seeks out those different from yourself or someone who would rather stick to his or her own kind?

___

4. What do you see as the advantages and disadvantages of each approach?

_____

_____

_____

_____

Step 3: Applying It to Work

Think about a time when you had to work with someone or a group of people outside one of your social identity groups. Describe the situation and reflect on what worked well and what did not.

_____

_____

_____

_____

It is common for leaders to lead groups made up of subgroups whose members see each other as different. Creating a cohesive group when subgroups have negative attitudes about each other requires reducing the negative intergroup attitudes *and* promoting positive intergroup attitudes (Pittinsky, 2009).

To examine your skill level in creating cohesive groups of followers out of subgroups who have negative attitudes about each other, answer the questions below as they pertain to your past experiences with social identity conflict:

1. When leading diverse groups with negative attitudes about one another or in-group members working with out-group members, what percentage of the time do you encourage them to do the following?

   _____ Recategorize the other (see them as us) through a superordinate identity or goal that binds us to them

   _____ Decategorize the other (see the other as an individual rather than as a member of a group)

   _____Emphasize dual identities (simultaneously emphasize the senses of them, us, and an overarching we)

2. What approach do you tend to use and why?

   _____

   _____

   _____

   _____

3. What other tactics could you use?

   _____

   _____

   _____

   _____

Cultural Intelligence (CQ)

exercise
SIX

Objective: This exercise is designed for you to examine each factor of your cultural intelligence (CQ) for leadership effectiveness: motivational CQ, cognitive CQ, metacognitive CQ, and behavioral CQ.

Key concepts: cultural intelligence (CQ), motivational CQ, cognitive CQ, metacognitive CQ, behavioral CQ

Relevant cases: 1, 2, 3, 4, 5, 12

Relevant Chapter
- Chapter 7: Cultural Intelligence: A Pathway for Leading in a Rapidly Globalizing World

Time required: Approximately 30 minutes

Learning Outcomes

1. Define cultural intelligence and the following factors: motivational CQ, cognitive CQ, metacognitive CQ, and behavioral CQ.
2. Describe how cultural intelligence factors impact leadership effectiveness in different settings.

Materials
- Pen/pencil

When to use: In the beginning of a session dealing with cross-cultural leadership. If it is a session that focuses on developing CQ, the exercise can be repeated after the session as well.

Physical setting: A room in which participants can comfortably be seated at tables and complete the questionnaire.

INSTRUCTIONS

Leaders need all four CQ capabilities to be effective; thus this exercise gives you an opportunity to examine each factor of your cultural intelligence:

Motivational CQ

How motivated are you to interact with diverse others despite challenges or conflict that may occur? How much enjoyment do you get out of working with others from different cultures? What are the barriers, if any, that prohibit you from readily interacting with diverse others? Answer these questions and jot down a few ways in which you might improve and eliminate any barriers.

_____

_____

_____

Cognitive CQ

How much do you know about other cultures? List any common business and social practices that you are aware of for the following cultures (if there are other cultures with which you work, you may want to include them in the list):

South Africa_____

_____

Japan_____

_____

China_____

_____

Brazil_____

_____

Saudi Arabia_____

_____

Spain_____

_____

United States_____

_____

Metacognitive CQ

If you are presented with a challenge of either garnering support from your diverse colleagues who are from very different contexts from your own or else risking failure to meet a major goal, what *must* you do within your presentation to your colleagues to elicit their support? What strategies must you use to ensure success? How will you evaluate your progress?

_____

_____

_____

Behavioral CQ

Assess your verbal and nonverbal actions by revisiting the cultures from the Cognitive CQ section. List verbal and nonverbal behaviors that would be appropriate/inappropriate in each of the above cultures. Think about your ability to modify these actions when necessary. Which practices are well developed? Which skills need to be enhanced?

_____

_____

_____

SELF-EXAMINATION AND REFLECTION

1. Based on what you now know about your cultural intelligence, how can you use each of the four factors of CQ to be more effective in cross-cultural and multicultural situations

_____

_____

_____

_____

2. List four specific things you can do to enhance your leadership capabilities in this rapidly globalizing world. What has worked in the past, and what must you do differently?

_____

_____

_____

_____

3. Why is cultural intelligence a necessary ability for leading effectively in a diverse working environment? Please explain.

_____

_____

_____

For more information on CQ, how to assess CQ, and how to enhance CQ, go to http://culturalq.com.

Your Leadership Practices

exercise **SEVEN**

Objective: The goal of this exercise is for you to explore your own responses to social identity conflict and to identify the leadership practices you typically prefer or expect an organization to use when managing social identity conflict.

Key concepts: leadership practices, social identity conflict, cross-group relationships, preferred social identity, conflict management behavior.

Relevant cases: 1, 3, 4, 5, 6, 9, 10, 11, 12, 13

Relevant Chapter
- Chapter 4: Leadership Practices Across Social Identity Groups

Time required: Approximately 15 to 20 minutes

Learning Outcomes
1. Identify leadership practice preferences for managing social identity conflict.
2. Articulate and apply the steps in the Leadership Response Cycle.

Materials
- Pen/pencil
- Calculator

When to use: Fairly deep into a session dealing with leadership across differences or managing workplace diversity.

Physical setting: A room in which participants can comfortably be seated at tables and complete the questionnaire.

119

INSTRUCTIONS

How do you typically respond to cross-group relationships and conflict at work? Complete the assessment below to identify your preferences for managing social identity conflict.

Review each of the items listed below. For those items that best describe your underlying beliefs about what the organization's role in managing cross-group relationships should be, score them with a **3**. For those items that somewhat describe your beliefs, score them with a **2.** For those items that do not describe your beliefs at all, score them with a **1**. After you have scored each item, total the scores under each approach and divide by the number of items. The approach that has the largest score is typically the one you prefer and is how you believe organizations should manage cross-group relationship conflict.

3 = I usually prefer this approach

2 = I sometimes prefer this approach

1 = I rarely, if ever, prefer this approach

Direct and Control Organization Characteristics

- ☐ Policies punishing discrimination and harassment
- ☐ Performance management systems that emphasize feedback, rewards, and punishment
- ☐ Formalized conflict management procedures providing a structure for complaints
- ☐ Staffing policies emphasizing mission and protecting organization boundaries
- ☐ Published code of conduct
- ☐ Organize work so groups are separated
- ☐ Intranet decision-making system to allow for input throughout the system

Total/7 items = _____

Hands-Off **Organization Characteristics**

- ☐ Doing nothing; letting the situation resolve on its own
- ☐ Denial of a problem
- ☐ Blame the victim
- ☐ Venting of emotion without taking action
- ☐ Emphasize only professional identities; do not recognize or encourage other identities

Total/5 items = _____

Cultivate and Encourage **Organization Characteristics**

- ☐ Diversity/sensitivity/cultural training and education to increase awareness of value of diversity
- ☐ Encouraging contact across groups/decategorization
- ☐ Creating a shared identity/recategorization
- ☐ Creating affinity groups/subcategorization
- ☐ Cross-cutting groups; creating diverse work teams
- ☐ Whole system interventions
- ☐ Creating boundary-crossing or bridging roles
- ☐ Climate of respect
- ☐ Apology and acceptance of apology
- ☐ Encouragement of individual initiative to resolve problems and conflicts
- ☐ Mentoring to facilitate integration of non-dominant groups
- ☐ Creation of a "safe" format for discussing conflict that promotes questioning, challenging debate, and open discussion

Total/12 items = _____

SELF-EXAMINATION AND REFLECTION

1. Do you prefer the Direct and Control, Hands-Off, or Cultivate and Encourage approach?

   _____

2. Have you used any of the three approaches in your leadership practices? Which ones did you use, and what was the outcome?

   _____
   _____
   _____
   _____

3. What actions/examples, if any, are missing from each group of characteristics?

   _____
   _____
   _____
   _____

4. If general steps are followed, an organization or individual can typically work toward preventing similar conflicts. In your past experience, have you or your organization followed the steps in the Leadership Response Cycle below, before responding to a conflict?

   a. Assess the situation

   b. Clarify your message

   c. Identify realistic expectations

5. Can you think about ways to improve your response by using the steps in the Leadership Response Cycle? The full cycle includes six steps: (1) Assess the Situation; (2) Clarify Your Message; (3) Identify Realistic Expectations; (4) Decide and Take Action; (5) Monitor Reactions, Act Again if Needed; and (6) Learn and Share.

Examining Your Leadership Networks

exercise **EIGHT**

Objective: In this exercise, you'll reflect on your own leadership network and the benefits of networking with individuals from different social identity groups. Having a strong and diverse network exposes you to different perspectives and provides you with access to information from different sources.

Key concepts: leadership networking, social identity groups
Relevant cases: 2, 5, 6, 7, 11, 13

Relevant Chapters
- Chapter 4: Leadership Practices Across Social Identity Groups
- Chapter 9: Miasma: The Dynamics of Difference

Time required: Approximately 1 hour

Learning Outcomes
1. Describe the benefits of networking with others from different social identity groups.
2. Identify strategies to enhance one's networks and become more effective at leadership networking.

Materials
- Flip-chart paper or notepaper
- Pen/pencil

When to use: Any time in a session dealing with diversity and leadership.

Physical setting: A room large enough for participants to work with flip-chart paper on large tables or on the floor.

INSTRUCTIONS

Step 1: Mapping Your Leadership Network

On a blank piece of flip-chart paper (or notepaper), draw large circles representing groups or individuals with whom you regularly interact or depend on to "get things done" at work. These can be people within or external to the organization. Likely categories of people to include are superiors, peers, direct reports, mentors, advisors, etc. You may also want to include the connections between the different individuals and groups among themselves with dotted or dashed rules.

Step 2: Examining Your Network

Examine your network and note the following:

- Where do you go to get information?

- Where do you go to get advice?

- Where do you go to get support?

- Whom do you trust?

- Who do you think trusts you?

- Are there certain types of people with whom you have a strong connection?

- Are there certain types of people not represented or with whom you have a weak connection?

___

Step 3: Applying a Social Identity Lens to Your Network

1. To what extent does the composition of your network "look like" your organization in terms of the different social identity groups?

___

2. To what extent does the composition of your network "look like" your customer or client base in terms of the different social identity groups?

___

3. To what extent does the composition of your network "look like" your community in terms of the different social identity groups?

___

4. Are members of different social identity groups under-represented or not represented at all? If so, which groups are they? What are the potential consequences of not being connected?

___

Step 4: Leveraging Your Leadership Network

Having connections to different social identity groups provides important insights into differences as well as lessons about building relationships and making alliances. Networking is essential to effective leadership. Leaders who are skilled networkers have access to people, information, and resources to help solve problems and create opportunities. Leaders who neglect their networks are missing out on a critical component of their roles as leaders. While having a diverse network may sound like something that is good to do, if you do not take the time to really think about the benefits of having a strong/diverse network or the consequences of not having a strong/diverse network, you probably will not be motivated to do much about it. So take a few moments to consider your experiences with your network, describe the value to you of networking, and identify ways to expand your network.

1. How has networking with different identity groups helped or hurt you professionally?

_____

_____

_____

_____

2. Describe situations in which networking with different identity groups helped you accomplish your work or got in the way of doing work.

_____

_____

_____

_____

3. What opportunities have you potentially missed by not networking with different identity groups?

_____

_____

_____

_____

4. What work-related goals or expectations are connected with a need to network with different identity groups?

5. How would you benefit by networking with different identity groups?

6. What steps can you take to build a more diverse network?

Tips for Building a Diverse Network

- Join professional organizations and seek out interest groups that will connect you with diverse perspectives.
- Ask questions about other people's experiences and listen (without judgment).
- Attend business events and community functions that will connect you with diverse perspectives.
- Become a member of an advisory board or volunteer with organizations that will increase your exposure to different perspectives.
- Invest yourself in the relationship, Try to give more than you receive.

Taking a New Perspective

exercise
NINE

Objective: The purpose of this exercise is to guide you through a "fieldwork" exercise, in an attempt to develop a deeper understanding of and empathy for a social identity group to which you do not belong.

Key concept: social identity
Relevant cases: 1 through 13

Relevant Chapters
- Chapter 1: Social Identity: Understanding the In-Group/Out-Group Group Phenomenon
- Chapter 2: Triggers of Social Identity Conflict
- Chapter 6: Approaches to Difference: Allophilia and Xenophobia
- Chapter 8: Social Justice and Dignity
- Chapter 9: Miasma: The Dynamics of Difference

Time required: At least 1 hour prior to activity and 1 hour post-activity; length of chosen activity will vary

Learning Outcome
1. Appreciate another social identity group's perspectives and experiences.

Materials
- Notepaper or a journal
- Pen/pencil

When to use: Almost at the end of a fairly long training period on leading across difference.

INSTRUCTIONS

Step 1: Identifying a Group

Identify a social identity group to which you do not belong. You may want to choose a group you know very little about and/or a group that you anticipate working closely with in the future (or perhaps are already working with). For example, if you often work with people from another country, but do not know much about the customs or history of that country, you may want to choose that national group. To the extent possible, think about why you want to know more about that group and what specifically it would be helpful to know.

Step 2: Identifying an Experience

Next, determine what kind of fieldwork would expose and/or immerse you in the traditions and norms of the group you selected. An extreme example could be traveling to a foreign country. However, it is probably more practical (and feasible) to think of something closer to home such as attending the services of a different religious group, visiting a low-income area within your community, or attending a celebratory or ceremonial event from another group. There are two extremes of conducting fieldwork. On one side you immerse yourself in the situation, fully participating in activities to the maximum extent possible. On the other hand, you may be more comfortable acting as an observer or witness, especially if your participation would be offensive to others and/or against your value system.

Below are some guidelines to apply when selecting your fieldwork:

- Select a situation or event that you are genuinely interested in learning about.
- If you tend to be associated with majority or dominant groups, you might want to put yourself in a situation in which you are the minority or non-dominant group.

- Make sure it is feasible for you to participate in or witness the situation.
- Get permission, an invitation, or at a minimum be sure you won't be seen as an intruder. For instance, don't assume you can just "drop in" on a religious ceremony.
- Consider your safety. Do not take unnecessary risks! While hanging out in a crime-ridden area alone after dark may open you to a new perspective, it also puts you in harm's way.

Step 3: Documenting the Experience

First, take some time to jot notes about what you expect to see or experience prior to beginning your fieldwork. This will allow you to more fully reflect on your experience. Next, you will need to document your fieldwork in order to make sense of it later. You can either do this in the moment (for example, by recording it or by taking notes—if it is legal and acceptable) or after the fact (for example, by journaling about it). If you decide to document after the fact, do so as quickly as possible after the experience while details and emotions are still fresh. Below are some tips about the kind of things to document:

- Describe the situation.
- What is/was your reaction to the situation?
- How did others respond to you?
- What surprised you about your reaction or the reaction of others to you?
- What did you notice about leadership and power dynamics?
- How did you feel about the experience?

Step 4: Making Sense of It All

A very rich experience will still not make you an expert in any social identity group; recognize your experience for what it is—a very small taste of something different. For example, spending a night or two in a cardboard box or living for a dollar a day in a city may illuminate challenges and perspectives associated with homelessness and poverty, but they do not qualify as having the full experience of being homeless or poor. However, chances are you know more than you did before the experience. Respond to the questions to prompt deeper learning.

1. How do your thoughts prior to taking part in the field experience compare to the actual experience? Were you accurate? Were there any surprises? What did you learn that was new?

   _____

   _____

   _____

   _____

   _____

   _____

   _____

2. Do you feel differently about the social identity group now than you did before? How valuable was this experience for you? What goals can you set for yourself to make any necessary changes in you and in your ability to develop empathy for other social identity groups outside of your own?

   _____

   _____

   _____

   _____

   _____

   _____

   _____

3. If someone were to do fieldwork based on one of *your* identities, what do you think the person would discover? What situations or events do you think reveal the most about you?

PART FOUR
Group and Paired Exercises

The following exercises are designed for at least two people. Group size recommendations are based on medium-sized groups with one facilitator. If additional facilitators are available, larger group sizes may be accommodated. Exercises 1 through 8 link back to the previous individual exercises with corresponding numbers; most of the exercises need to be used in combination with a part of or an entire individual exercise.

As noted at the beginning of this guide, facilitators will likely work with one of the three types of groups described below. Recommendations are provided within each exercise in regard to the type of group the exercise is best suited for.

Type 1: groups in which people do not know each other.

Type 2: groups in which people know each other, but there is tension between them.

Type 3: groups in which participants know and like/trust each other, at least to some extent.

Seeking Another Perspective on Social Identity

exercise ONE

Objective: The goal of this exercise is to help individuals understand how others might perceive them in general and as leaders.

Key concepts: social identity, given identity, chosen identity, core identity, leadership, multiple identities, simultaneity of identities, identity mapping, life roles.

Relevant cases: all cases

Relevant Chapters
- Chapter 1: Social Identity: Understanding the In-Group/Out-Group Group Phenomenon
- Chapter 4: Leadership Practices Across Social Identity Groups

Time required: Approximately 60 to 80 minutes (10 minutes to brief; 20 minutes to complete identity maps if participants have not already done so; 30 minutes to establish partners, share identity maps, and provide one another with feedback; 20 minutes to debrief).

Group size: 12 to 60 participants (to be grouped into dyads)

Group type: This exercise is primarily recommended for group type 3, however, recommendations for use with group types 1 and 2 are provided below. Use trust-building exercises prior to pairing as necessary.

Learning Outcomes

1. Understand different perspectives on one's social identity.
2. Challenge assumptions about others' social identities.
3. Describe how social identity can help or hinder the ability to make connections with others.

Materials

- Each participant will need his or her completed identity map from Individual Exercise 1
- Flip chart and markers

When to use: At any time during a session.

Physical setting: A room in which participants can comfortably be seated at tables, view their identity maps, and walk around talking to other participants.

PAIRED ACTIVITY INSTRUCTIONS

1. Ask participants to choose someone they trust and whose opinions they value to be their partners in this activity because the activity involves the sharing of identity maps to gain another perspective. *Note*: If participants do not feel comfortable sharing their complete identity maps because they do not know each other well or know each other but there is tension between them, advise them to choose only the information they feel comfortable sharing and to discuss it verbally with their partners.

2. Tell participants that their partners may or may not see their maps the same way they do. In fact, it will be more interesting if the other person has a different perspective. Remind the group that there are no right or wrong interpretations. Instruct them to discuss the following with their partners (you may want to post these on a flip chart):

    - Aspects of your identity that you believe help you make connections with people at work
    - Aspects of your identity that you believe get in the way of making connections with people at work

3. Next, partners should ask the following questions of each other (again, you may want to post these):

- Are you surprised to see anything on my map?
- Are there aspects of me that you think have an impact on how others perceive me that I have not included on my map?

GROUP DEBRIEFING INSTRUCTIONS

In the larger group, ask for volunteers to share the new perspectives they have about themselves. Ask them if, in taking part in this exercise, they learned anything that will improve their understanding of and relationships with people different from themselves.

Note that participants can also share their social identity maps with others in the larger group and compare similarities and differences. There may be more communalities than differences within a group. This comparison gives the group an opportunity to interact and share with one another, and might be an ideal entry point into the discussion of similarities and difference.

Your Experience with Triggers

exercise TWO

Objective: This exercise is designed to engage the group in a discussion about triggering events and to use their colleagues to help identify alternative solutions for responding to them.

Key concepts: triggers, social and power conflict, differential treatment, assimilation, insults/humiliating acts, different values, simple contact

Relevant cases: all cases

Relevant Chapters
- Chapter 2: Triggers of Social Identity Conflict
- Chapter 3: Organizational Faultlines

Time required: 35 to 60 minutes (5 minutes to brief; 10 minutes to complete the Triggers table if not already completed; 10 to 15 minutes for group sharing; 10 minutes to debrief group; 20 minutes for paired activity).

Group size: Approximately 12 to 60 participants

Group type: This exercise is recommended for all group types. The paired activity portion of this exercise is primarily recommended for group type 3, but recommendations for use with group types 1 and 2 are provided.

Learning Outcomes
1. Articulate the role values play in responding to triggering events.
2. Identify alternative ways to respond to triggering

143

Materials

- Each participant will need his or her completed Triggers table from Individual Exercise 2
- Pen/pencil

When to use: In the middle or toward the end of a session following activities on social identity conflict or during sessions that help identify general diversity information.

Physical setting: A room in which participants can comfortably be seated at tables and view their Trigger tables, and large enough to walk around and talk to each other.

GROUP INSTRUCTIONS

Ask participants to take a few moments to complete the "Your Experience with Triggers" form if they haven't already done so (refer to Individual Exercise 2). After they have completed the exercise, ask for volunteers to share with the group what they wrote in the Experience and Values boxes.

Engage the group in a discussion about the triggering events that were discussed to try to gain a deeper understanding of the social identity issues. Next, ask for alternative ways the situations could have been handled. Finally, ask whether others have had similar experiences so the group can compare and contrast experiences.

PAIRED ACTIVITY INSTRUCTIONS

Participants can break out in groups of two and share their social identity conflict experiences one-on-one. *Note*: If participants fall into group types 1 or 2, remind them that they may limit what they share to only details that they are comfortable sharing. Use trust-building exercises prior to pairing as necessary.

It would be more effective if the dyads are more different in social identity than similar. This exercise gives individuals an opportunity to start sharing and learning across difference and might be a very good springboard to discuss how culture and values can influence behavior and perceptions. Also, how culture and values can influence leader decisions and follower expectations, which is explored in more depth in Exercise 4: Cultural Values.

Identifying Faultlines

exercise
THREE

Objective: This exercise is designed to help groups collaborate to identify potential faultlines in their work groups or other teams.

Key concepts: faultlines
Relevant cases: 5, 6, 8, 9, 10, 11, 12, 13

Relevant Chapters
- Chapter 3: Organizational Faultlines
- Chapter 4: Leadership Practices Across Social Identity Groups

Time required: Approximately 30 to 60 minutes (10 minutes to brief and allow participants to complete the Faultline form; approximately 30 to 50 minutes to review the leadership practices from Chapter 4 and have the full-group discussion).

Group size: Approximately 12 to 40 participants.

Group type: This exercise is recommended for group types 1 and 3.

Learning Outcomes
1. Explain faultline dynamics in groups or teams.
2. Identify potential faultlines in groups or teams.

Materials
- Each participant needs his or her Faultline form from Individual Exercise 3
- Pen/pencil
- Flip chart and markers

When to use: At any time during a session.

Physical setting: A room in which participants can comfortably be seated at tables.

145

GROUP DEBRIEFING INSTRUCTIONS

Ask each participant to refer to his or her completed Faultline form as you discuss the following questions as a group:

1. Do any of the differences in the team/group co-occur, such that members are different in terms of more than one characteristic and subgroups are similar in terms of more than one characteristic? For example, all of the women are older and all of the men are younger.

2. Explain that research suggests that groups that are very similar and groups that contain a lot of differences are less likely to experience faultlines, because similar groups do not have many differences and groups with a great deal of difference have so many differences that subgroups tend not to form. However, it has also been noted that the relevance and prominence of the differences influence the degree to which faultlines may be experienced. Ask for volunteers to respond to this research based on their experiences in their work groups and other teams.

3. Ask for volunteers to share specific experiences, including the context in which the group or team was (or is working) and how clear the task at hand was and how clear the roles of various group or team members were.

4. (If you assigned the Leadership Practices Across Social Identity Groups chapter) Ask participants to discuss the practices that were used, or could have been used, in the examples given (you may want to flip chart these practices to get an idea about the practices that are most often used).

Cultural Values

exercise
FOUR

Objective: This exercise is designed to connect participants with their diverse colleagues to garner their reactions about individual decision making based on cultural values.

Key concepts: cultural values, decision making, autonomy vs. embeddedness, egalitarianism vs. hierarchy, harmony vs. mastery
Relevant cases: 2 through 13

Relevant Chapters
- Chapter 5: Cultural Values
- Chapter 10: Leader Values and Authenticity

Time required: 45 to 65 minutes (5 minutes to brief; 20 minutes to complete the cultural values chart if necessary; 20 minutes for subgroup discussions; 20 minutes for group debriefing).
Group size: Approximately 40 to 60 participants (in subgroups of 4 or 6).
Group type: This exercise is recommended for all group types.

Learning Outcomes
1. Articulate the role one's preferred cultural values play in decision making, and how values impact others.
2. Recognize how cultural value orientations impact decision making.

Materials

- Each participant needs his or her Cultural Values chart from Individual Exercise 4
- Pen/pencil
- Flip chart and markers

When to use: At any time during a session.

Physical setting: A room in which participants can comfortably be seated at tables and reflect. If the session is in a casual setting, encourage participants to do the subgroup work outdoors or some other comfortable place.

SUBGROUP INSTRUCTIONS

1. If participants have not already done so, ask them to take a few moments to complete the Cultural Values chart. (Refer to Individual Exercise 4.)
2. Divide participants into small groups of four or six with varied social identities. Ask each participant to bring his or her completed Cultural Values chart and discuss the following within the groups (you may want to place these items on a flip chart):
   - One decision you made and the influence your cultural values had on that decision.
   - How the decisions you made would have affected the others in your subgroup.
   - Which value orientation(s) are most closely related to the decision you made based on your cultural values.

GROUP DEBRIEFING QUESTIONS

After each person has had an opportunity to share a decision he or she has made within the subgroup, bring the full class back together and ask for volunteers to answer the questions below and share their subgroup discussions.

1. Would you make the same decision or choice again, given what you have learned about cultural values?
2. Which values were easiest to identify? Which were the hardest to identify?
3. As you recognized the cultural values that impacted your decision making, how did that make you feel?

Approaches to Difference

exercise **FIVE**

Objective: This exercise is designed for pairs of different social identities to work together and learn about two new orientations/perspectives (allophilia and xenophobia) that explain one's orientation to difference and the working relationships that are impacted. Partners should discuss their encounters when working with others outside of their social identity groups and brainstorm ways to improve future encounters.

Note: This activity uses many of the same elements as Individual Exercise 5, but in a group format, so you would likely use either the Individual or this Group exercise, but not both with the same group.

Key concepts: xenophobia, allophilia, social identity

Relevant cases: 6, 9, 11, 13

Relevant Chapter
- Chapter 6: Approaches to Difference: Allophilia and Xenophobia

Time required: Approximately 60 minutes (20 minutes to read the Approaches to Difference chapter or provide a brief overview of the chapter and allow participants to select image; 5 minutes to assign partners; 15 minutes to answer the paired activity questions and the assessment; 20 minutes for group debriefing).

Group size: Approximately 12 to 40 participants (these participants will be in pairs).

Group type: This exercise is recommended for all group types.

Learning Outcomes

1. Define xenophobia and allophilia.
2. Identify one's orientation to social identity differences.
3. Develop ways to improve future encounters with individuals from different social identity groups.

Materials

- Magazines or Internet access, from which an image can be selected
- Flip-chart paper
- Pen/pencil

When to use: In the middle or toward the end of a session following activities on social identity conflict or in sessions that help identify workplace diversity.

Physical setting: A room large enough for participants to work on large tables or the floor to page through the magazines, and to walk around and talk to each other.

INSTRUCTIONS

1. Ask participants to read the Approaches to Difference chapter from the casebook. Then ask them to leaf through images (in magazines or online) and identify pictures that represent how they feel when they encounter someone very different from themselves, in general. For example, show participants the image of puzzle pieces. (This image is also included in Individual Exercise 5 in the casebook.) Explain that this image could represent an individual's sense that by encountering others he or she has more perspectives to consider (and thus more puzzle pieces) and sees a bigger picture, which creates feelings of excitement and fulfillment. However, the same image could represent an individual's sense that things are coming apart or are more divided—making it difficult to know what fits together and creating feelings of anxiety and perhaps resentment.

Picture of Puzzle Pieces

2. Assign each person a partner of a different social identity (race, gender, ethnicity, age, or other social identities that you are aware of).

3. Ask participants to look at the images they selected and think about what they represent in terms of how they approach differences. Partners should then discuss the following with one another (place these questions on a flip chart):

    - How your object represents your approach to difference
    - Expectations you have about the outcome of encounters with others very different from yourself and why
    - The feelings that tend to surface when you work with someone very different from yourself. Is it something positive? Uncomfortable, but necessary? Or something you'd rather avoid altogether if possible?
    - Do you generally and actively seek out those different from yourself, or would you rather stick with your own kind? Why or why not?
    - If partners had not been assigned, would you have chosen someone from a different social identity group as a partner? Why or why not?

4. Explain to the group that it is common for leaders to lead groups made up of subgroups whose members see each other as different.

5. Post the question below on a flip chart, and ask participants to individually assess their skill level in creating cohesive groups of followers out of subgroups who have negative attitudes about each other by answering the question as it pertains to their past experiences with social identity conflict:

When leading diverse groups with negative attitudes about one another, or in-group members working with out-group members, what percentage of the time have you been able to lead them to do the following:

_____ Recategorize the other (see them as us) through a superordinate identity or goal that binds us to them,

_____ Decategorize the other (see the other as an individual rather than as a member of a group)

_____ Emphasize dual identities (simultaneously emphasize the senses of them, us, and an overarching we).

6. After everyone has finished, bring the group back together and ask for volunteers to share the discussion they had with their partners and the answers to the creating cohesive groups question. Ask the participants whether they feel that one or more of these methods did or would have worked for their past conflicts. Why or why not?

Cultural Intelligence (CQ)

exercise **SIX**

Objective: This exercise is designed for individuals to learn from others from different social identity groups by providing one another with feedback based on their knowledge about various countries (social, political, economic, and historical issues).

Key concepts: cultural intelligence (CQ), cognitive (CQ)
Relevant cases: 1, 2, 3, 4, 5, 12

Relevant Chapter
- Chapter 7: Cultural Intelligence: A Pathway for Leading in a Rapidly Globalizing World

Time required: 60 to 70 minutes (10 minutes to complete the Cognitive CQ form if they haven't already done so; 15 minutes for country highlight review; 10 minutes for paired activity; 20 minutes for group debriefing; 15 minutes to complete Goal Planning Sheet).

Group size: 40 participants (divided into 20 pairs)
Group type: This exercise is recommended for all group types.

Learning Outcomes
1. Define cultural intelligence and the following factors: motivational CQ, cognitive CQ, metacognitive CQ, and behavioral CQ.
2. Describe how cultural intelligence factors impact leadership effectiveness in different settings.
3. Create a plan to enhance one's CQ.

Materials
- Each participant will need his or her completed cognitive CQ section of Individual Exercise 6

153

- Literature that provides an overview of the culture of several different countries (Recommendation): Gannon, M. (2004). *Understanding global cultures: Metaphorical journeys through 28 nations, clusters of nations and continents.* Thousand Oaks, CA: Sage
- A Goal Planning sheet for each participant
- Pen/pencil

When to use: In the beginning of a session dealing with cross-cultural leadership. If it is a session that focuses on developing CQ, the exercise can be repeated after the session as well.

Physical setting: A room in which participants can comfortably be seated at tables and complete the questionnaire and also sit around tables in pairs.

PAIRED ACTIVITY INSTRUCTIONS

1. Ask each participant to refer to his or her completed Cognitive CQ section from Individual Exercise 5.

2. Next, briefly review the country highlights with the class. You may want to create a PowerPoint slide or some other teaching material that reviews cultural aspects of various countries. Readings in the Gannon book or some other literature can also be assigned to be read prior to or during the class.

3. After the review, ask participants to choose partners from a different social identity group to discuss what they have learned from the country highlights. Ask them to also discuss what they know about other countries from life experience, work, travel, research, and so forth in regard to the countries' cultures and practices (social, political, economic, and historical issues).

GROUP DEBRIEFING QUESTIONS

1. As a group, ask participants to discuss how their CQ has been impacted as a result of what they've learned from the country highlights and from spending time with their partners (from different social identity groups).

2. Ask participants to discuss the steps they must take to ensure they are able to lead successfully in a rapidly globalizing world.

3. (Optional) Give participants Goal Planning Sheets and ask them to map out one goal (as a result of this activity) that they intend to tackle within the next thirty days. Preview the Sample Goal Planning Sheet so participants understand what is desired.

SAMPLE GOAL PLANNING SHEET

Goal Statement: *To learn from others from different social identity groups*

Start Date: January 18

End Date: November 2

Benefits That Will Accrue for Me and the Organization	Obstacles to Be Overcome: Preventative and Contingent	What Must Be Done to Achieve This Goal?	Timed Activities: Dates and Times for Each
A greater understanding of my diverse colleagues and an enhanced comfort level while interacting with others different from myself.	Increased productivity and less potential for conflict between diverse colleagues.	Preventative: Reluctance to engage with others not like me. Contingent: Routine opportunities to interact with diverse others.	I must learn more about other cultures by reading about diverse cultures, attending various cultural events. I must make a conscious effort to engage with diverse others, including speaking to them in the hallway, even if I haven't already developed a relationship with them. Weekly: Learn something specific about a new culture, including what the group appreciates and what offends them.

Accountability Partner(s)	Available Resources Within and Outside of the Organization	Methods for Measuring Progress	Sacrifice That Will Be Required
Kelly, Lize, Dave	Within: Diverse colleagues, company library, and other electronic and visual media, in house diversity training. Outside: Cultural events. Relevant public seminars and workshops.	Successful collaborations and project work with diverse others.	Coming out of my comfort zone.

GOAL PLANNING SHEET

Goal Statement: _____

_____

Start Date: _____   End Date: _____

Benefits That Will Accrue for Me and the Organization	Obstacles to Be Overcome: Preventative and Contingent	What Must Be Done to Achieve This Goal?	Timed Activities: Dates and Times for Each

Cultural Intelligence (CQ)　**157**

Accountability Partner(s)	Available Resources Within and Outside of the Organization	Methods for Measuring Progress	Sacrifice That Will Be Required

Your Leadership Practices

exercise **SEVEN**

Objective: The purpose of this exercise is to shed light on diverse preferences for managing social identity conflict.

Key concepts: leadership practices, social identity conflict, cross-group relationships, preferred social identity, conflict management behavior

Relevant cases: 1, 3, 4, 5, 6, 9, 10, 11, 12, 13

Relevant Chapter
- Chapter 4: Leadership Practices Across Social Identity Groups

Time required: Approximately 70 to 80 minutes (10 minutes to brief and have participants complete form if they have not already done so; 10 minutes to poll and assign groups; 10 minutes for small group discussion on preferences; 30 minutes for full-group reporting; 20 minutes for group debriefing).

Group size: 12 to 40 participants

Group type: This exercise is recommended for all group types.

Learning Outcomes
1. Identify leadership practice preferences for managing social identity conflict.
2. Articulate the strengths and weaknesses of various leadership practices.

Materials
- Each participant will need his or her completed Cross-Group Relationships and Conflict Assessment from Individual Exercise 7
- Pen/pencil

When to use: In the middle or toward the end of a session dealing with leadership across differences or managing workplace diversity.

Physical setting: A room in which participants can comfortably be seated at tables and complete the questionnaire and enough space so that participants can walk around and talk to each other. If the session is in a casual setting, encourage participants to do the subgroup work outdoors or find another comfortable place.

SUBGROUP INSTRUCTIONS

1. Ask participants to complete Individual Exercise 7 if they have not already done so.
2. Take a poll and determine how many people fall into each of the three categories (approaches) for managing cross-group relationships.
3. Next, form subgroups that contain a mix of preferred approaches (Direct and Control, Hands-Off, and Cultivate and Encourage preferences).
4. Ask the subgroup members to discuss among themselves why they prefer specific principles.

FULL-GROUP INSTRUCTIONS

1. Bring the class back together and ask for a spokesperson from each group to report on what they have learned from their group discussions.
2. Then ask for individual volunteers to describe their preferences to the rest of the group. Participants should explain in detail why their particular preference works well. Try to find at least one proponent of each of the three approaches.
3. Ask the groups to discuss the strengths and weakness of the various approaches.
4. Have participants respond to the following questions:
   - What happened when you heard that others chose a different option for managing cross-group relationships than you? How did that make you feel?
   - Is there one best way of dealing with conflict in cross-cultural relationships?

Examining Leadership Networks

exercise
EIGHT

Objective: This exercise is designed for work groups within an organization to reflect on their current leadership networks/teams and the benefits of networking within their teams and with individuals from other work groups within their organization who may be from different social identity groups (gender, race, class, etc.) or from different departments (a human resources group vs. a facilities management group; an accounting group vs. a group of employees who work in the warehouse).

Key concepts: leadership networking, social identity groups
Relevant cases: 2, 5, 6, 7, 11, 13

Relevant Chapters
- Chapter 4: Leadership Practices Across Social Identity Groups
- Chapter 9: Miasma: The Dynamics of Difference

Time required: Approximately 45 to 65 minutes (5 minutes to brief, gather into work groups, and distribute flip-chart paper; 20 to 30 minutes for groups to complete Steps 1, 2, and 3; 20 to 30 minutes to complete Step 4 as a full-group discussion).

Group size: 12 to 60 participants (participants will work within their current work groups within the organization)

Group type: This exercise is recommended for group type 2, particularly work groups within an organization who have experienced intergroup tension

161

Learning Outcomes

1. Describe the collective benefits of networking with different social identity groups.
2. Identify strategies to enhance a group's networks and to become more effective at leadership networking.

Materials

- Flip-chart paper
- Markers
- Notepaper
- Pen/pencil

When to use: Any time during a session dealing with diversity and leadership.

Physical setting: A room large enough for participants to work with flip-chart paper on large tables or the floor and to break up in different smaller groups.

INSTRUCTIONS

Step 1: Mapping Your Leadership Network

Explain to participants that having a strong and diverse network exposes them to different perspectives and provides them with access to information from different sources. Ask them to gather together with their work team members (the people they work with every day). Give each group a sheet of paper from the flip chart and a marker and ask them to select someone within their group to do the writing and drawing.

Ask each team to draw large circles representing groups or individuals with whom they regularly interact or depend on to "get things done" at work. These can be people within or external to the organization: likely categories of people to include are other groups they depend on to do their work.

Step 2: Examining Your Network

Ask participants to examine their networks and discuss the following within their groups (place these questions on a flip chart):

- Where do team members typically go to obtain information?
- Where do they go to get advice?
- Where do they go for support?

- Who do the team members trust?
- Who do you think trusts your group?
- Are there certain types of people or groups with whom they have a strong connection?
- Are there certain types of people or groups not represented or with whom you have a weak connection?

Groups may choose to place their responses on their flip charts or simply designate note-takers.

Step 3: Applying a Social Identity Lens to Your Network

Ask the teams to discuss the following questions among their work teams (networks):

- Does the composition of your network "look like" your organization in terms of the different social identity groups?
- Does the composition of your network "look like" your customer or client base in terms of the different social identity groups?
- Does the composition of your network "look like" your community in terms of the different social identity groups?
- Are members of different social identity groups underrepresented or not represented at all? If so, which groups are they and what are the potential consequences of not being connected?

Step 4: Leveraging Your Leadership Network

Bring the full group back together and explain the following:

> Having connections to different social identity groups provides important insights into differences as well as lessons about building relationships and making alliances. Networking is essential to effective leadership. Leaders who are skilled networkers have access to people, information, and resources to help solve problems and create opportunities. Leaders who neglect their networks are missing out on a critical component of their role as leaders. While having a diverse network may sound like something that is good to do, if you do not take the time to really think about the benefits of

having a strong/diverse network or the consequences of not having a strong/diverse network, you probably will not be motivated to do much about it.

Ask for volunteers from different work teams to respond to the questions below. Ask them to provide specific examples, encouraging them to speak to situations in which individuals from different work groups have or have not worked with one another:

- How has networking with different identity groups helped or hurt your work teams?
- Are there situations in which networking with different identity groups helped you or your work team accomplish your work or got in the way of doing work?
- What opportunities has your work team potentially missed by not networking with different identity groups?
- What work-related goals or expectations are connected with a need to network with different identity groups?
- How would you or your team benefit by networking with different identity groups?
- What steps can you or your work team take to build a more diverse network?

Exploring Mental Models of Leadership

exercise
NINE

Objective: This exercise is designed to help individuals examine diverse perspectives of effective leadership and understand how mental models of leadership influence expectations.

Key concepts: leadership, leadership stereotypes, mental models, social identity
Relevant cases: 1, 3, 4, 8, 10, 13

Relevant Chapter
- Chapter 5: Cultural Values

Time required: Approximately 50 to 85 minutes, depending on group size (5 minutes to brief and choose object; 2 minutes each to share individual notions of effective leadership; 20 minutes to debrief)
Group size: 12 to 30 participants
Group type: This exercise is recommended for all group types.

Learning Outcomes
1. Identify different perspectives on effective leadership.
2. Articulate the influence social identity has on one's mental model of leadership.
3. Describe how mental models of leadership influence expectations of leaders.

Materials
- Notepaper
- Pen/pencil
- Various objects, toys, and images

When to use: At the beginning of a session or as an icebreaker.

Physical setting: A room large enough so that participants can comfortably be seated at tables and stroll about.

GROUP ACTIVITY INSTRUCTIONS

1. Most people have some idea or mental model of leadership in mind when they think of effective leadership. Ask participants to select an image or an object that conveys effective leadership to them. It is a good idea to have various objects or images in the room from which individuals can choose if they'd like. For example, LEGO, slinky, yo-yo, rocking horse, a selection of action figures, fighter jet, airplane, star, clock, etc. Let participants know, however, that it is not necessary to choose an object or image that is present. They can simply describe an image that conveys effective leadership.

2. Ask each participant to share his or her own notions of effective leadership (1 or 2 minutes each).

3. Once everyone has spoken, ask the group to identify what themes emerge in terms of common ideas about effective leadership. What images or ideas about leadership were not similar? In what ways might aspects of one's social identity influence one's mental model of leadership? In what ways do our mental models of leadership influence our expectations of leaders? How can leaders be effective in situations when there are different ideas about effective leadership (or different expectations of how they will be effective leaders)?

4. If time permits, ask participants to choose objects or images that represent their notion of *ineffective* leadership. Again, ask them to share their ideas with the class within 1 or 2 minutes per person. Follow up with comparisons and contrasts of effective and ineffective leadership.

Using Film in the Classroom to Illustrate Difference

exercise **TEN**

Objective: The purpose of this exercise is to illustrate difference by engaging learners in media exercises using film and guided discussions.

Key concepts: difference, digital media, purposeful viewing, reframe
Relevant cases: N/A

Relevant Chapters
- Facilitator's Guide: Chapter 4: Using Film to Illustrate Different Perspectives
- Choose chapter(s) in the casebook that are relevant to the film or the theoretical aspects that you want to illustrate through the use of film.

Time required: Depends on the length of the film.
Group size: No more than 60 participants
Group type: This exercise is recommended for all group types.

Learning Outcome
1. This approach can be used to meet a variety of learning outcomes. Facilitators must identify a learning outcome appropriate to their session and then apply this approach with that outcome (or outcomes) in mind.

Materials
- Audio/video devices and materials
- Pen/pencil/paper

- Handout or list of "Purposeful Viewing" questions
- Flip chart

When to use: Any time during a session.

Physical setting: A room in which participants can comfortably be seated and that can be darkened.

INSTRUCTIONS (TIPS)

1. Consult your organization's code of best practices for using digital media before engaging learners in a viewing exercise. Note that nonprofit institutions generally approve using film for educational purposes in a classroom setting.

2. Select films that are cinematically interesting, theoretically revealing, and that connect well with the current curriculum or discussion topic. For a list of film suggestions, see the Using Film to Illustrate Different Perspectives chapter in this guide.

3. If time permits, show the entire film. If you are unable to show the full film, show as much as possible, focusing on the screen most relevant to the topic.

4. Purposeful viewing: Give participants an assignment to find examples, themes, or behaviors in the film that translate to the topic being studied.

5. Debrief exercise that addresses the assigned questions (place these questions on a flip chart to be displayed only after the movie is over). Encourage learners to discuss as many illustrations of difference observed as possible and try to obtain multiple perspectives. If the class is focusing on a single topic such as different interpretations of loyalty, show short clips from different films and give each participant the same assignment. Because the films demonstrate different behaviors, they will be able to compare and contrast their observations.

6. Allow participants to watch the film as a group rather than alone at home because they typically obtain an additional benefit from the shared experience.

RESOURCES

Note: An asterisk indicates a most relevant/recommended resource.

Addressing Diversity in Organizations

Argyris, C. (1993). *Knowledge for action. A guide to overcoming barriers to organizational change.* San Francisco: Jossey-Bass.

*Brewer, M. (1995). Managing diversity: The role of social identities. In S. Jackson & M. Ruderman (Eds.), *Diversity in work teams* (pp. 47–68). Washington, DC: American Psychological Association.

Bhawuk, D.P.S. (1997). Leadership through relationship management: Using the theory of individualism and collectivism. In R.W. Brislin & K. Cushner (Eds.), *Improving intercultural interactions: Modules for cross-cultural training programs, 2*. Thousand Oaks, CA: Sage.

Cameron, K.S., & Quinn, R.E. (1988). Organizational paradox and transformation. In R.E. Quinn & K.S. Cameron (Eds.), *Paradox and transformation: Toward a theory of change in organization and management* (pp. 1–18). Cambridge, MA: Ballinger.

Cox, T. Jr. (1993). *Cultural diversity in organizations: Theory, research and practice.* San Francisco: Berrett-Koehler.

Cox, T. Jr. (2001). *Creating the multicultural organization: A strategy for capturing the power of diversity.* San Francisco: Jossey-Bass.

Cox, T. Jr., & Beale, R. (1997). *Developing competency to manage diversity.* San Francisco: Berrett-Koehler.

Dovidio, J.F., Gaertner, S.L., & Bachman, B.A. (2001). Racial bias in organizations: The role of group processes in its causes and cures. In M.E. Turner (Ed.), *Groups at work: Theory and research* (pp. 415–444). Mahwah, NJ: Lawrence Erlbaum Associates.

Ensari, N.K., Christian, J., & Miller, N. (2006). Workplace diversity and group relations: An overview. *Group Processes & Intergroup Relations*, 9(4), 459–466.

Fatehi, K. (2007). *Managing internationally: Succeeding in a culturally diverse world.* Thousand Oaks, CA: Sage.

Harvey, C.P., & Allard, M.J. (Eds.). (2005). *Understanding and managing diversity: Readings, cases, and exercises* (3rd ed.). Upper Saddle River, NJ: Prentice-Hall.

Jackson, S.E., & Associates (1992). *Diversity in the workplace*. New York: Guilford Press.

Plummer, D.L. 2003. *Handbook of diversity management: Beyond awareness to competency-based learning*. Lanham, MD: University Press of America, Inc.

Allophillia

Pittinsky, T.L. (2005). Allophilia and intergroup leadership. In N.N. Huber & M. Walker (Eds.), *Building leadership bridges: Emergent models of global leadership*. College Park, MD: International Leadership Association.

Pittinsky, T.L., & Maruskin, L. (2008). Allophilia: Beyond prejudice. In S. J. Lopez (Ed.), *Positive psychology* (Vol. 2, pp. 141–148). Westport, CT: Praeger.

Pittinsky, T.L., & Montoya, R.M. (2009). Is valuing equality enough? Equality values, allophilia, and social policy support for multiracial individuals. *Journal of Social Issues*, 65(1), 151–163.

Pittinsky, T.L., Rosenthal, S.A., & Montoya, R.M. (forthcoming). Attitudes beyond tolerance: Allophilia in intergroup relations. In L. Tropp & R. Mallett (Eds.), *Beyond prejudice reduction: Pathways to positive intergroup relations*. Washington, DC: American Psychological Association.

Center for Creative Leadership Tools

http://cclve.blogspot.com/2007/04/introduction-to-visual-explorer.html

Cultural Intelligence

*Ang, S., & Van Dyne, L. (Eds.). *Handbook on cultural intelligence: Theory, measurement and applications* (pp. xi–xiv). New York: M E Sharpe, Inc.

Early, P.C., & Ang, S. (2003). *Cultural intelligence: Individual iteractions across cultures*. Palo Alto, CA: Stanford University Press.

Early, P.C., & Peterson, R.S. 2004. The elusive cultural chameleon: Cultural intelligence as a new approach to intercultural training for the global manager. *Academy of Management Learning and Education*, 3(1), 100–115.

Livermore, D. (2009). *Leading with cultural intelligence: The new secret to success*. New York: AMACOM.

Ng, K.Y., Ang, S., & Van Dyne, L. (2009). Beyond international experience: The strategic role of cultural intelligence for executive selection of international human resource management. In P.R. Sparrow (Ed.), *Handbook of international human resource research: Integrating people, process, and context*. Oxford: Blackwell.

Ng, K.Y., Van Dyne, L., & Ang, S. (2009). Developing global leaders: The role of international experience and cultural intelligence. In W.H. Mobley, Y. Wang, & M. Li (Eds.), *Advances in global leadership*. New York: JAI.

Van Dyne, L., & Ang, S. (2008). The sub-dimensions of the four-factor model of cultural intelligence. Technical Report. East Lansing, MI: Cultural Intelligence Center.

Van Dyne, L., Ang, S., & Koh, C. (2009). Cultural intelligence: Measurement and scale development. In M.A. Moodian (Ed.), *Contemporary leadership and intercultural competence: Exploring the cross-cultural dynamics within organizations* (pp. 233–254). Thousand Oaks, CA: Sage.

Van Dyne, L., Ang, S., & Nielsen, T.M. (2007). Cultural intelligence. In S. Clegg & J. Bailey, (Eds.), *International encyclopedia of organization studies* (pp. 345–350). Thousand Oaks, CA: Sage.

Cultural Values

Hofstede, G. (2001). *Culture's consequences: Comparing values, behaviours, institutions, and organizations across nations.* Thousand Oaks, CA: Sage.

Hofstede, G., & Hofstede, G.-J. (2004). *Cultures and organizations: Software of the mind.* New York: McGraw-Hill.

House, R., Hanges, P., Javidan, M., Dorfman, P., & Gupta, V. (Eds). (2004). *Leadership, culture and organizations: The globe study of 62 societies.* Thousand Oaks, CA: Sage.

Leung, K., & Ang, S. (2008). Culture, organizations, and institutions: An integrative review. In R.S. Bhagat & R.M. Steers (Eds.), *Cambridge handbook of culture, organizations and work* (pp. 23–45). New York: Cambridge University Press.

Sagiv, L., & Schwartz, S.H. (2007). Cultural values in organizations: Insights for Europe. *European Journal of International Management*, 1, 176–190.

Schwartz, S.H. (1999). Cultural value differences: Some implications for work. *Applied Psychology: An International Review*, 48, 23–47.

Schwartz, S.H. (1992). Universals in the content and structure of values: Theoretical advances and empirical tests in 20 countries. *Advances in Experimental Social Psychology*, 25, 1–65.

Schwartz, S.H. (2004). Mapping and interpreting cultural differences around the world. In H. Vinken, J. Soeters, & P Ester (Eds.), *Comparing cultures: Dimensions of culture in a comparative perspective* (pp. 43–73). Leiden, The Netherlands: Brill.

*Schwartz, S.H. (2006). A theory of cultural value orientations: Explication and applications. *Comparative Sociology*, 5, 137–182.

Schwartz, S.H., & Bilsky, W. (1987). Toward a universal psychological structure of human-values. *Journal of Personality and Social Psychology*, 53(3), 550–562.

Schwartz, S.H., & Sagie, G. (2000). Value consensus and importance: A cross-national study. *Journal of Cross-Cultural Psychology*, 31(4), 465–497.

Triandis, H.C. (1989). The self and social behavior in differing cultural contexts. *Psychological Review*, 96(3), 506–520.

Triandis, H.C. (1990). Cross-cultural studies of individualism and collectivism. In J. Bremen (Ed.), *Nebraska symposium on motivation* (pp. 41–133). Lincoln: University of Nebraska Press.

Triandis, H.C. (1995). *Individualism and collectivism*. Boulder, CO: Westview Press.

Triandis, H.C., & Bhawuk, D.P.S. (1997). Culture theory and the meaning of relatedness. In P. C. Earley & M. Erez (Eds.), *New perspectives on international industrial/organizational psychology* (pp. 13–52). New York: New Lexington Free Press.

Triandis, H.C., Chan, D., Bhawuk, D.P.S., Iwao, S., & Sinha, J.B.P. (1995). Multi-method probes of allocentrism and idiocentrism. *International Journal of Psychology*, 30(4), 461–48.

Faultlines

*Lau, D.C., & Murnighan, J.K. (1998). Demographic diversity and faultlines: The compositional dynamics of organizational groups. *Academy of Management Review*, 23, 325–340.

Lau, D.C., & Murnighan. J.K. (2005). Interactions within groups and subgroups: The effects of demographic faultlines. *Academy of Management Journal*, 48, 645–659.

Li, J., & Hambrick, D. (2005). Factional groups: A new vintage on demographic faultlines, conflict, and disintegration in work teams. *Academy of Management Journal*, 48, 794–813.

Thatcher, S.M.B., Jehn, K.A., & Zanutto, E. (2003). Cracks in diversity research: The effects of diversity faultlines on conflict and performance. *Group Decision and Negotiation*, 12, 217–241.

Williams, K.Y., & O'Reilly, C.A. (1998). Demography and diversity in organizations: A review of 40 years of research. *Research in Organizational Behavior*, 20, 77–140.

Gender at Work

Booysen, L. (1999, Winter/Spring). Male and female managers: Gender influences on South African managers in retail banking. *South African Journal of Labour Relations*, 23(2&3), 25–35.

Booysen, L., & Nkomo, S.M. (2006). Think manager—think (fe)male: A South African perspective. *The International Journal of Interdisciplinary Social Sciences*, 1(2), 23–33.

Eagly, A.H., & Carli, L.L. (2003). The female leadership advantage: An evaluation of the evidence. *The Leadership Quarterly*, 14, 807–834.

Eagly, A.H., & Carli, L.L. (2003). Finding gender advantage and disadvantage : Systematic research integration is the solution. *The Leadership Quarterly*, 14, 851–859.

Vecchio, R.P. (2002). Leadership and gender advantage. *The Leadership Quarterly*, 13(6), 643–671.

Vecchio, R.P. (2003). In search of gender advantage. *The Leadership Quarterly*, 14, 835–850.

Helpful Websites

www.adl.org. This website contains resources of the Anti-Defamation League (ADL), whose purpose is to oppose anti-Semitism and all forms of bigotry and to defend democratic ideals and civil rights.

www.allophilia.org. This website has all the latest information on allophilia research, including contact information for copies of the Allophilia Scale. Interchange on creating and nurturing allophilia in workplaces, schools, neighborhoods, nations, and the world.

www.culturalq.com The Cultural Intelligence Center (CQC) website contains resources dedicated to improving the understanding of cultural intelligence (CQ).

www.pbs.org/wgbh/pages/frontline/shows/schools/testing/ Testing, Teaching, Learning

www.tolerance.org. The Teaching Tolerance website is sponsored by the Southern Poverty Law Center and is dedicated to reducing prejudice, improving intergroup relations, and supporting equitable school experiences for children. Teaching Tolerance provides free educational materials, including downloadable curricula for teachers and other classroom activities.

[The] Impact of Differences on Organizational Outcomes

Bezrukova, K., Jehn, K.A., Thatcher, S., & Zanutto, E. (in press). A field study of group faultlines, team identity, conflict, and performance in diverse groups. *Organization Science*.

Brickson, S. (2000). The impact of identity orientation on individual and organizational outcomes in diverse settings. *Academy of Management Review*, 25(1), 82–101.

Christian, J., Porter, L.W., & Moffitt, G. (2006). Workplace diversity and group relations: An overview. *Group Processes & Intergroup Relations*, 9(4), 459–466.

Ely, R.J., & Thomas, D.A. (2001). Cultural diversity at work: The effects of diversity perspectives of work group processes and outcomes. *Administrative Science Quarterly*, 46, 229–273.

Graves, L.M., Ohlott, P.J., & Ruderman, M.N. (2007). Commitment to family roles: Effects on managers' attitudes and performance. *Journal of Applied Psychology*, 9(1), 44–56.

Harrison, D.A., Price, K.H., & Bell, M.P. (1998). Beyond relational demography: Time and the effects of surface- and deep-level diversity on work group cohesion. *Academy of Management Journal*, 41, 96–107.

Jehn, K.A. (1995). A multimethod examination of the benefits and detriments of intragroup conflict. *Administrative Science Quarterly*, 40, 256–282.

Milliken, F.J., & Martins, L.L. (1996). Searching for common threads: Understanding the multiple effects of diversity in organizational groups. *Academy of Management Review*, 21, 402–433.

Thatcher, S.M.B., Jehn, K.A., & Zanutto, E. (2003). Cracks in diversity research: The effects of diversity faultlines on conflict and performance. *Group Decision and Negotiation*, 12, 217–241.

van Knippenberg, D., De Dreu, C.K.W., & Homan, A.C. (2004). Work group diversity and group performance: An integrative model and research agenda. *Journal of Applied Psychology*, 89, 1008–1022.

In-Group/Out-Group Behaviors

Van den Berghe, P.L. (1999). Racism, ethnocentrism, and xenophobia: In our genes or in our memes? In K. Thienpont & R. Cliquet (Eds.), *In-group/out-group behaviour in modern societies: An evolutionary perspective* (pp. 21–33). Brussels: NIDI CBGS.

Van der Dennen, J.M.G. (1987). Ethnocentrism and in-group/out-group differentiation: A review of the literature. In V. Reynolds, V. Falger, & I. Vine (Eds.), *The sociobiology of ethnocentrism: Evolutionary dimensions of xenophobia, discrimination, racism, and nationalism* (pp. 1–47). Athens, GA: University of Georgia Press.

Van der Dennen, J.M.G. (2004). Self-cooperation, loyalty structures, and proto-ethnocentrism in inter-group agonistic behavior. In F. Salter (Ed.), *Welfare, ethnicity and altruism: New findings and evolutionary theory* (pp. 195–231). London: Frank Cass.

Leadership

Avolio, B.J., & Gardner, W.L. (2005). Authentic leadership development: Getting to the root of positive forms of leadership. *Leadership Quarterly, 16*, 315 .

Avolio, B.J., Gardner, W.L., Walumbwa, F.O., Luthans, F., & May, D.R. (2004). Unlocking the mask: A look at the process by which authentic leaders impact follower attitudes and behaviors. *Leadership Quarterly, 15*(6), 801–823.

Avolio, B.J., & Luthans, F. (2006). *The high impact leader: Moments matter in accelerating authentic leadership development*. New York: McGraw-Hill.

Avolio, B.J., Luthans, F., & Walumbwa, F.O. (2004). Authentic leadership: Theory-building for veritable sustained performance. Working paper. Gallup Leadership Institute.

Bass, B.M. (1985). *Leadership and performance beyond expectations*. New York: The Free Press.

Burke, C.S., Sims, D.E., Lazzara, E.H., & Salas, E. (2007). Trust in leadership: A multi-level review and integration. *The Leadership Quarterly, 18*(6), 606–632.

Burns, J.M. (1978). *Leadership*. New York: Harper & Row.

Gardner, W.L., Avolio, B.J., & Walumbwa, F. (Eds.). (2005). *Authentic leadership theory and practice: Origins, effects and development*. New York: JAI.

*Heifetz, R. (1998). *Leadership without easy answers*. Boston: Harvard Business School Press.

House, R., Hanges, P., Javidan, M., Dorfman, P., & Gupta, V. (Eds). (2004). *Leadership, culture and organizations: The globe study of 62 societies*. Thousand Oaks, CA: Sage.

MacDonald, H.A., Sulsky, L.M., & Brown, D.J. (2008). Leadership and perceiver cognition: Examining the role of self-identity in implicit leadership theories. *Human Performance, 21*(4), 333–353.

Measures or Assessments

Standards for Educational and Psychological Testing. (2nd ed.). (1999). Washington, DC: American Educational Research Association.

Walker, A., & Smither, J.W. (1999). A five-year study of upward feedback: What managers do with their results matters. *Personnel Psychology*, 52(2), 393–423.

Paradox and Polarity Management

Handy, C. (1994). *The age of paradox*. Cambridge, MA: Harvard Business School Press.
Johnson, B. (1996). *Polarity management*. Amherst, MA: HRD Press.
Smith, K., & Berg, D. (1987). *Paradoxes of group life*. San Francisco: Jossey-Bass.

[The] Role of Leadership in Addressing Diversity in Organizations

Chrobot-Mason, D., & Ruderman, M.N. (2004). Leadership in a diverse workplace. In M.S. Stockdale & F.J. Crosby (Eds.), *The psychology and management of workplace diversity* (pp. 100–121). Malden, MA: Blackwell.

*Ernst, C., & Chrobot-Mason, D. (manuscript in preparation). *Boundary spanning leadership*. New York: McGraw-Hill.

*Ernst, C.T., Hannum, K.M., & Ruderman, M.N. (2010). Developing intergroup leadership. In C.D. McCauley, E. Van Velsor, & M.N. Ruderman (Eds.), *Handbook of leadership development*. San Francisco: Jossey-Bass.

Homan, A.C., & Jehn, K.A. (in press). How leaders can make diverse groups less difficult: The role of attitudes and perceptions of diversity. In S. Schuman (Ed.), *The handbook for working with difficult groups: How they are difficult, why they are difficult, and what you can do*. San Francisco: Jossey-Bass.

Kearney, E., & Gebert, D. (2009). Managing diversity and enhancing team outcomes: The promise of transformational leadership. *Journal of Applied Psychology*, 94(1), 77–89.

*Pittinsky, T.L. (Ed.). (2009). *Crossing the divide: Intergroup leadership in a world of difference*. Boston: Harvard Business School Press.

Stone, D., Patton, S., & Heen, S. (1999). *Difficult conversations: How to discuss what matters most*. New York: The Penguin Group.

Same-Sex Orientation Policies and Practices

Colgan, F., Creegan, C., McKearney, A., & Wright, T. (2007). Equality and diversity policies and practices at work: Lesbian, gay and bisexual workers. *Equal Opportunities International*, 26(6), 590–609.

Social Identity

*Abrams, D., & Hogg, M.A. (2004). Metatheory: Lessons from social identity research. *Personality and Social Psychology Review*, 8(2), 98–106.

*Allport, G.W. (1954). *The nature of prejudice*. Reading, MA: Addison-Wesley.

Ashforth, B.E., & Mael, F. (1989). Social identity theory and the organization. *Academy of Management Review*, 14(1), 20–39.

*Brewer, M. (1995). Managing diversity: The role of social identities. In S. Jackson & M. Ruderman (Eds.), *Diversity in work teams* (pp. 47–68). Washington, DC: American Psychological Association.

Crenshaw, K. (2005). Mapping the margins: Intersectionality, identity politics, and violence against women of color (1994). *Violence against women: Classic papers* (pp. 282–313). Auckland: New Zealand: Pearson Education New Zealand.

*Dovidio, J.G., Glick, P., & Rudman, L.A. (2005). On the nature of prejudice: Fifty years after Allport. Malden, MA: Blackwell.

Essed, P. (2001). Multi-identifications and transformations: Reaching beyond racial and ethnic reductionisms. *Social Identities, 7*(4), 493–509.

*Haslam, S.A. (2001). *Psychology in organizations: The social identity approach.* London: Sage.

Haslam, S.A., van Knippenberg, D., Platow, M J., & Ellemers, N. (Eds.). (2003). *Social identity at work: Developing theory for organizational practice.* Philadelphia, PA: Psychology Press.

Hill, J. (2000). *Becoming a cosmopolitan: What it means to be a human in the new millennium.* Lanham: MD: Rowman & Littlefield.

*Hogg, M.A., & Terry, D.J. (2000). Social identity and self-categorization processes in organizational contexts. *Academy of Management Review, 25*(1), 121–140.

Hornsey, M.J. (2008). Social identity theory and self-categorization theory: A historical overview. *Social and Personality Psychology Compass, 2*(1), 204–222.

*Nkomo, S.M., & Stewart, M. (2006). Diverse identities in organizations. In C.S. Hardy & W. Nord (Eds.), *The Sage handbook of organisational studies* (2nd ed.). London: Sage.

Stryker, S. (2007). Identity theory and personality theory: Mutual relevance. *Journal of Personality, 75*(6), 1083–102.

*Tajfel, H., & Turner, J.C. (1986). The social identity theory of intergroup behavior. In S. Worchel & Austin (Eds.), *Psychology of inter-group relations* (2nd ed.) (pp. 7–24). Chicago: Nelson-Hall.

van Knippenberg, D., & Haslam, S. (2003). Realizing the diversity dividend: Exploring the interplay between identity, ideology and reality. In S. Haslam, D. van Knippenberg, M. Platow, & N. Ellemers (Eds.), *Social identity at work: Developing theory for organizational practice* (pp. 61–77). New York: Psychology Press.

Social Identity Conflict

Bezrukova, K., Jehn, K.A., Thatcher, S., & Zanutto, E. (2004, September). A field study of group faultlines, team identity, conflict, and performance in diverse groups. *Journal of Organizational Behavior, 25*(6), 703–729.

Chrobot-Mason, D., Ruderman, M.N., Ernst, C., & Weber, T.J. (in press). Leading on unstable ground: How triggers activate social identity faultlines. *Human Relations.*

*Chrobot-Mason D., Ruderman, M.N., Weber, T.J., Ohlott, P.J., & Dalton, M.A. (2007). Illuminating a cross-cultural leadership challenge: When identity groups collide. *The International Journal of Human Resource Management, 18*(11), 2011–2036.

Cockburn, C. (1998). *The space between us: Negotiating gender and national identities in conflict.* London: Zed Books.

Jehn, K.A. (1994). Enhancing effectiveness: An investigation of advantages and disadvantages of value-based intragroup conflict. *International Journal of Conflict Management*, 5, 223–238.

Jehn, K.A. (1995). A multi-method examination of the benefits and detriments of intra-group conflict. *Administrative Science Quarterly*, 40, 256–282.

Jehn, K.A., Northcraft, G.B., & Neale, M.A. (1999). Why differences make a difference: A field study of diversity, conflict, and performance in workgroups. *Administrative Science Quarterly*, 44, 741–763.

Tajfel, H., & Turner, J. (2001). An integrative theory of intergroup conflict. *Intergroup relations: Essential readings* (pp. 94–109). New York: Psychology Press.

Thatcher, S.M.B., Jehn, K.A., & Zanutto, E. (2003). Cracks in diversity research: The effects of diversity faultlines on conflict and performance. *Group Decision and Negotiation*, 12, 217–241.

[Addressing] Social Identity Conflict

Graetner, S.L., & Dovidio, J.F. (2000). *Reducing inter-group bias: The common in-group identity model*. Philadelphia, PA: Psychology Press.

Gratton, L., Voigt, A., & Erickson, T. (2007). Bridging faultlines in diverse teams. *MIT Sloan Management Review*, pp. 22–29.

Hampden-Turner, C., & Trompenaars, F. (2000). *Building cross-cultural competence: How to create wealth from conflicting values*. Hoboken, NJ: John Wiley & Sons.

*Hewstone, M., & Brown, R. (1986). Contact is not enough: An intergroup perspective on the contact hypothesis. In M. Hewstone & R. Brown (Eds.), *Contact and conflict in intergroup encounters* (pp. 1–44). Oxford: Blackwell.

Homan, A.C., & Jehn, K.A. (in press). How leaders can make diverse groups less difficult: The role of attitudes and perceptions of diversity. In S. Schuman (Ed.), *The handbook for working with difficult groups: How they are difficult, why they are difficult, and what you can do*. San Francisco: Jossey-Bass.

Homan, A.C., van Knippenberg, D., Van Kleef, G.A., & De Dreu, C.K.W. (2007). Bridging faultlines by valuing diversity: The effects of diversity beliefs on information elaboration and performance in diverse work groups. *Journal of Applied Psychology*, 92, 1189–1199.

Kossek E.E., Lobel S.A., & Brown, J. (2005) Human resource strategies to manage workforce diversity. In A. Konrad, P. Prasad, & J.K. Pringle (Eds.), *Handbook of workplace diversity* (pp. 53–74). London: Sage.

Rothman, J. (1997). *Resolving identity-based conflict in nations, organizations, and communities*. San Francisco: Jossey-Bass.

Structural Discrimination

Bell, E.E., & Nkomo, S.M. (2001). Gender and cultural diversity in the workplace. In L. Diamant & J. Lee (Eds.), *The psychology of sex, gender and jobs: Issues and solutions*. Westport, CT: Praeger.

Cox, T. Jr., & Nkomo, S.M. (2001). Race and ethnicity: An update and analysis. In R.T. Golembiewski (Ed.), *Handbook of organizational behavior* (2nd ed.) (pp. 255–286). New York: Marcel Dekker.

Whiteness in South Africa

Booysen, L. (2001, Summer). The duality in South African leadership: Afrocentric or Eurocentric. *South African Journal of Labour Relations, 25*(3&4), 36–64.

Booysen, L. (2007). Barriers to employment equity implementation and retention of blacks in management in South Africa. *Southern African Journal of Labour Relations, 31*(1), 47–71.

Booysen, L. (2007). Societal power shifts and changing social identities in South Africa: Workplace implications. *Southern African Journal of Economic and Management Sciences, 10*(1), 1–20.

Booysen, L., Kelly, C., Nkomo, S.M., & Steyn, M. (2007). Rethinking the diversity paradigm: South African practices. *International Journal on Diversity in Organisations, Communities & Nations, 7*(4), 1–10.

Booysen, L., & Nkomo, S.M. (2007). The tea incident: Racial division at Insurance Incorporated—A teaching case. *International Journal on Diversity in Organisations, Communities & Nations, 7*(5), 97–106.

Horwitz, F.M., Browning, V., Jain, H., & Steenkamp, A.J. 2002. Human resource practices and discrimination in South Africa: Overcoming the apartheid legacy. *International Journal of Human Resource Management, 13*(7), 1105–1118.

Steyn, M.E. (2002). *Whiteness in the rainbow: The subjective experience of loss of privilege in the new South Africa*. In C.H. Hamilton, L. Huntley, N. Alexander, A.S. Guimaraes, & W. James (Eds.), *Beyond racism: Race and inequality in Brazil, South Africa, and the United States*. Atlanta, GA: Lynne Rienner Publishers.

Soudien, C. (1998). Equality and equity in South African education: Multiculturalism and change. In M. Cross & Z. Mkwanazi Twala (Eds.), *Unity, diversity and reconciliation: A debate on the politics of curriculum in South Africa*. Cape Town: Juta.

REFERENCES

Alderfer, C.P., & Smith, K.K. (1982). Studying intergroup relations embedded in organizations. *Administrative Science Quarterly*, *27*, 35–65.

Anti-Defamation League. (2004). *Establishing safe learning environments when discussing controversial issues.* www.adl.org/education/brown_2004/safe_environment.

Atkinson, E. (2007). Speaking with small voices: Voice, resistance and difference. In M. Reiss, R. DePalma, & E. Atkinson (Eds.), *Marginality and difference in education and beyond* (pp. 15–29). Stoke on Trent, UK: Trentham Books.

Avigdor, A., Braun, D., Konkin, J., Kuzmycz, D., & Ferdman, B.M. (2007). Workgroup inclusion, diversity, and performance. Paper presented at the Annual Meeting of the Academy of Management, Philadelphia.

Baxter Magolda, M.B. (1998). Developing self-authorship in young adult life. *Journal of College Student Development*, *39*, 143–156.

Bentz, V., & Shapiro, J. (1998). *Mindful inquiry in social research*. Thousand Oaks, CA: Sage.

Bloom, B.S., & Krathwohl, D.R. (1956). *Taxonomy of educational objectives: The classification of educational goals, by a committee of college and university examiners. Handbook 1: Cognitive domain*. New York: Longmans.

Boler, M., & Zembylas, M. (2003). Discomforting truths: The emotional terrain of understanding difference. In P. Trifonas (Ed), *Pedagogies of difference: Rethinking education for social change* (pp. 110–136). New York: Routledge Falmer.

Bolman, L., & Deal, T. (1984). *Modern approaches to understanding and managing organizations*. San Francisco: Jossey-Bass.

Bolman, L., & Deal, T. (1991). *Reframing organizations: Artistry, choice and leadership*. San Francisco: Jossey-Bass.

Bowen, F., & Blackmon, K. (2003). Spirals of silence: The dynamic effects of diversity on organizational voice. *Journal of Management Studies*, *40*, 1393–1417.

Brickson, S. (2000). The impact of identity orientation on individual and organizational outcomes in demographically diverse settings. *Academy of Management Review*, *25*, 82–101.

Bushe, G.R. (2001). *Clear leadership: How outstanding leaders make themselves understood, cut through the mush, and help everyone get real at work*. Palo Alto, CA: Davies-Black.

Champoux, J.E. (1999). Film as a teaching resource. *Journal of Management Inquiry*, 8(2), 206–217.

Clemons, J., & Wolf, M. (1999). *Movies to manage by: Lessons in leadership from great films*. Chicago: Contemporary Books.

Cox, T. Jr. (2001). *Creating the multicultural organization: A strategy for capturing the power of diversity*. San Francisco: Jossey-Bass.

Creed, W.E.D., & Scully, M.A. (2000). Songs of ourselves: Employees' deployment of social identity in workplace encounters. *Journal of Management Inquiry*, 9, 391–412.

Davidson, M.N. (1999). The value of being included: An examination of diversity change initiatives in organizations. *Performance Improvement Quarterly*, 12, 164–180.

Davidson, M.N., & Ferdman, B.M. (2002). A matter of difference—Inclusion and power: Reflections on dominance and subordination in organizations. *The Industrial-Organizational Psychologist*, 40(1), 62–67.

DePalma, R. (2007). "She went too far": Civility, complaint and dialoguing with the other. In M. Reiss, R. DePalma, & E. Atkinson (Eds.), *Marginality and difference in education and beyond* (pp. 121–133). Stoke on Trent, UK: Trentham Books.

Edmondson, A.C. (1999). Psychological safety and learning behavior in work teams. *Administrative Science Quarterly*, 44, 350–383.

Ellison, R. (1952). *Invisible man*. New York: Random House.

Ely, R.J. (1995). The role of dominant identity and experience in organizational work on diversity. In S.E. Jackson & M.N. Ruderman (Eds.), *Diversity in work teams: Research paradigms for a changing workplace* (pp. 161–186). Washington, DC: American Psychological Association.

Ely, R.J., & Thomas, D.A. (2001). Cultural diversity at work: The effects of diversity perspectives on work group processes and outcomes. *Administrative Science Quarterly*, 46, 229–273.

Erwin, T.D. (1991). *Assessing student learning and development: A guide to the principles, goals, and methods of determining college outcomes*. San Francisco: Jossey-Bass.

Ferdman, B.M. (1997). Values about fairness in the ethnically diverse workplace. [Special Issue: Managing in a global context: Diversity and cross-cultural challenges]. *Business and the Contemporary World: An International Journal of Business, Economics, and Social Policy*, 9, 191–208.

Ferdman, B.M. (2003). Learning about our and others' selves: Multiple identities and their sources. In N. Boyacigiller, R. Goodman, & M. Phillips (Eds.), *Crossing cultures: Insights from master teachers* (pp. 49–61). London: Routledge.

Ferdman, B.M. (2004). The inclusive workplace. In G.N. Powell, (Ed.) *Managing a diverse workforce: Learning activities* (2nd. ed.) (pp. 165–168). Thousand Oaks, CA: Sage.

Ferdman, B.M. (2007a). Inclusion starts with knowing yourself. *San Diego Psychologist*, 22(4), 1, 5–6.

Ferdman, B.M. (2007b). Self-knowledge and inclusive interactions. *San Diego Psychologist*, *22*(5), 25–26.

Ferdman, B.M. (2009, Spring). ORG7330 Cultural Diversity in Organizations. Course syllabus, Alliant International University, San Diego.

Ferdman, B.M., Barrera, V., Allen, A., & Vuong, V. (2009, August). Inclusive behavior and the experience of inclusion. In B.G. Chung (Chair), What makes an organization inclusive: Measures, HR practices and climate. Symposium presented at the Annual Meeting of the Academy of Management, Chicago.

Ferdman, B.M., & Davidson, M.N. (2002). A matter of difference—Inclusion: What can I and my organization do about it? *The Industrial-Organizational Psychologist*, *39*(4), 80–85.

Ferdman, B.M., Katz, J., Letchinger, E., & Thompson, C.T. (2009). Inclusive behaviors and practices (Version 1.1). Manuscript in preparation, Institute for Inclusion (www.instituteforinclusion.org).

Fletcher, J. (2001). *Disappearing acts: Gender, power and relational practice at work*. Cambridge, MA: The MIT Press.

Foldy, E.G., Rivard, P., & Buckley, T.R. (2009). Power, safety, and learning in racially diverse groups. *Academy of Management Learning & Education*, *8*(1), 25–41.

Frost, P., Louis, M., Lundberg, C., & Martin, J. (Eds.). (1991). *Reframing organizational culture*. Thousand Oaks, CA: Sage.

Gable, R.K. (1986). *Instrument development in the affective domain*. Boston: Kluwer-Nijhoff.

Gallos, J.V. (1993). Teaching about reframing with films and videos. *Journal of Management Education*, *17*(1), 127–132.

Gasorek, D. (2000). Inclusion at Dun & Bradstreet: Building a high-performing company. *The Diversity Factor*, pp. 25–29.

Gilbert, J.A., & Ivancevich, J.M. (2000). Valuing diversity: A tale of two organizations. *Academy of Management Executive*, *14*(1), 93–105.

Halle, T.G., Kurtz-Costes, B., & Mahoney, J.L. (1997). Family influences on school achievement in low-income, African American children. *Journal of Educational Psychology*, *89*, 527–537.

Hannum, K.M., & Weber, T. (2005). New challenges in a changing world. *Leadership in Action*, *25*(2), 11–12.

Holvino, E., Ferdman, B.M., & Merrill-Sands, D. (2004). Creating and sustaining diversity and inclusion in organizations: Strategies and approaches. In M.S. Stockdale & F.J. Crosby (Eds.), *The psychology and management of workplace diversity* (pp. 245–276). Malden, MA: Blackwell.

Homan, A., & Jehn, K. (2010). Organizational faultlines. In K.M. Hannum, B. McFeeters, & L. Booysen (Eds.), *Leading across differences: Cases and perspectives* (pp. 87–94). San Francisco: Pfeiffer.

Hooks, B. (1994). *Teaching to transgress: Education as the practice of freedom*. New York: Routledge.

Hyter, M.C., & Turnock, J.L. (2005). *The power of inclusion: Unlock the potential and productivity of your workforce.* Mississauga, Ontario: Wiley Canada.

Issacs, W. (1999). *Dialogue and the art of thinking together.* New York: Currency.

Jandt, F.E. (2007). *An introduction to intercultural communication: Identities in a global community* (5th ed.). Thousand Oaks, CA: Sage.

Katz, J.H., & Miller, F.A. (1996). Coaching leaders through culture change. *Consulting Psychology Journal: Practice and Research, 48,* 104–114.

King, J.R., & Schneider, J.J. (1999). Locating a place for gay and lesbian themes in elementary reading, writing, and talking. In W. Letts & J.T. Sears (Eds.), *Queering elementary education: Advancing the dialogue about sexualities and schooling* (pp. 125–136). Lanham, MD: Rowman and Littlefield.

Kirkpatrick, D.L. (1994). *Evaluating training programs: The four levels.* San Francisco: Berrett-Koehler.

Kolb, D.A. (1999). *Learning style inventory, version 3.* Boston: Hay Group.

Kuh, G.D., Schuh, J.H., Whitt, E., & Associates. (1991). *Involving colleges: Successful approaches to fostering student learning and development outside the classroom.* San Francisco: Jossey-Bass.

Lovitts, B. (2001). *Leaving the ivory tower: The causes and consequences of departure from doctoral study.* Lanham, MD: Rowman & Littlefield.

Mankiller, W.P., & Wallis, M. (1993). *Mankiller: A chief and her people.* New York: St. Martin's Press.

Miller, F.A., & Katz, J.H. (2002). *The inclusion breakthrough: Unleashing the real power of diversity.* San Francisco: Berrett-Koehler.

Mor-Barak, M.E. (2005). *Managing diversity: Toward a globally inclusive workplace.* Thousand Oaks, CA: Sage.

Morgan, G. (1986). *Images of organization.* Thousand Oaks, CA: Sage.

National Council of Graduate Schools. (2008). Ph.D. completion project. www.cgsnet.org

Nkomo, S. (2010). Social identity: Understanding the in-group/out-group group phenomenon. In K.M. Hannum, B.B. McFeeters, & A.E. Booysen (Eds.). (2010). *Leading across differences: Cases and perspectives* (pp. 73–80). San Francisco: Pfeiffer.

Noonan, W.R. (2007). *Discussing the undiscussable: A guide to overcoming defensive routines in the workplace.* San Francisco: Jossey-Bass.

Parker, C.G., Frye, C.M., & Robinson, S.L. (2006). Images of diversity on the silver screen: Using full-length feature films to teach diversity and the management of differences, Paper is posted at DigitalCommons@University of Nebraska–Lincoln. http://digitalcommons.unl.edu/pocpwi1/1

Public Conversations Project. (2004). *Constructive conversations about challenging times: A guide to community dialogue.* Retrieved June 15, 2008, from www.publicconversations.org/

Quinn, R. (1988). *Beyond rational management: Mastering the paradoxes and competing demands of high performance.* San Francisco: Jossey-Bass.

Ruderman, M., Glover, S., Chrobot-Mason, D., & Ernst, C. (2010). Leadership practices across social identity groups. In K.M. Hannum, B.B. McFeeters, & A.E. Booysen (Eds.), *Leading across differences: Cases and perspectives* (pp. 95–114). San Francisco: Pfeiffer.

Sanford, N. (1962). Developmental status of the entering freshman. In N. Sanford (Ed.), *The American college* (pp. 253–282). Hoboken, NJ: John Wiley & Sons.

Shavelson, R.J., Roeser, R.W., Kupermintz, H., Lau, S., Ayala, C., Haydel, A., Schultz, S., Gallagher, L., & Quihuis, G. (2002). Richard E. Snow's remaking of the concept of aptitude and multidimensional test validity: Introduction to the special issue. *Educational Assessment*, 8(2), 77–99. Retrieved April 01, 2009, from www.informaworld.com/10.1207/S15326977EA0802_01.

Stone, D., Patton, S., & Heen S. (1999). *Difficult conversations: How to discuss what matters most*. New York: Penguin.

Storey, J. (1999). *Cultural consumption and everyday life*. London: Arnold.

Storey, J. (2007). Culture and hegemony. In M. Reiss, R. DePalma, & E. Atkinson (Eds.), *Marginality and difference in education and beyond* (pp. 3–14). Stoke on Trent, UK: Trentham Books.

Strayhorn, T.L., & Hirt, J.B. (2008). Social justice and student affairs work at minority serving institutions. In M.B. Gasman, B. Baez, & C.S.V. Turner (Eds.), *Understanding minority-serving institutions* (pp. 203–216). Albany: State University of New York Press.

Wasserman, I.C., Gallegos, P.V., & Ferdman, B.M. (2008). Dancing with resistance: Leadership challenges in fostering a culture of inclusion. In K.M. Thomas (Ed.), *Diversity resistance in organizations* (pp. 175–200). New York: Taylor and Francis.

Williams, R. (2006). The analysis of culture. In J. Storey (Ed.), *Cultural theory and popular culture: A reader* (3rd ed.) (pp. 32–40). London: Pearson.

ABOUT THE CONTRIBUTORS

Laurien Alexandre is professor and director of the doctoral program in leadership and change program at Antioch University. Her current areas of interest are higher education change and relational leadership.

Bernardo M. Ferdman is a professor at Alliant International University's Marshall Goldsmith School of Management. He consults, writes, speaks, and teaches on diversity and inclusion, multicultural leadership, Latinos/as in the workplace, and bringing one's whole self to work. (More details are available on his website, http://bernardoferdman.org.)

Emily R. Hoole is the director of the Evaluation Center at the Center for Creative Leadership. She specializes in evaluating the impact of custom leadership development and works with global Fortune 500 companies in the areas of individual leader development, leadership networks, coaching, and organizational transformation.

Terrell Strayhorn is an associate professor, special assistant to the provost, and director of the Center for Higher Education Research and Policy at The University of Tennessee, Knoxville. His research centers on issues of access, equity, race, and diversity in education, with a particular accent on racial and economic disparities in post-secondary education.

C*lemson Turregano* is director of government services for the Center for Creative Leadership. A former professor at the U.S. Naval War College and West Point, his current research focus is an edited work on different examples of mentoring.

ABOUT THE EDITORS

Belinda B. McFeeters is an independent contractor with faculty affiliations with the evaluation center at the Center for Creative Leadership, the Leadership Studies Ph.D. Program at North Carolina A&T State University, and the Leadership Development group at the N.C. Rural Economic Development Center. She is also a freelance writer for EBSCO Publishing. Belinda earned a Ph.D. in educational leadership and policy studies from Virginia Polytechnic Institute and State University. Her primary research, evaluation, and assessment focus is on leadership development (national and global) and diversity education. Belinda has authored or co-authored several articles, book chapters, and books on higher education, multicultural education, K-12 education, cross-cultural leadership, and sociological issues.

Kelly M. Hannum is manager of research for the EMEA Region at the Center for Creative Leadership. She holds a Ph.D. in educational research, measurement, and evaluation from the University of North Carolina at Greensboro. In addition to her work at CCL, Kelly has conducted research and evaluation projects with organizations in a variety of sectors and countries. She is a visiting faculty member at Catholic University's IESEG School of Management in Lille, France, and teaches graduate-level courses at the University of North Carolina at Greensboro. Her work has been published and presented internationally in a variety of venues. She is the recipient of the Marcia Guttentag award from the American Evaluation Association and Young Alumni Awards from the University of North Carolina at Greensboro and Guilford College.

Lize Booysen is a full professor, Leadership and Change, at Antioch University. Lize is an internationally recognized scholar in the field of diversity, race, gender, and leadership and a management consultant. She holds a doctorate in business leadership as well as master's degrees in clinical psychology, research psychology, and criminology, all with distinction. Prior to joining Antioch in 2009, Lize was full professor at the Graduate School of Business Leadership, University of South Africa, since 1992. She was also the editor of the *South African Journal of Labour Relations*. Some of Lize's many awards include the GLOBE Research Award (1997) and Best Academic Achievement, University of South Africa, (2004). She is also included as one of fifty role models for South African women and as leadership expert in the book *Inspirational Women @ Work* (Lapa Publishers, 2003).

Pfeiffer Publications Guide

This guide is designed to familiarize you with the various types of Pfeiffer publications. The formats section describes the various types of products that we publish; the methodologies section describes the many different ways that content might be provided within a product. We also provide a list of the topic areas in which we publish.

FORMATS

In addition to its extensive book-publishing program, Pfeiffer offers content in an array of formats, from fieldbooks for the practitioner to complete, ready-to-use training packages that support group learning.

FIELDBOOK Designed to provide information and guidance to practitioners in the midst of action. Most fieldbooks are companions to another, sometimes earlier, work, from which its ideas are derived; the fieldbook makes practical what was theoretical in the original text. Fieldbooks can certainly be read from cover to cover. More likely, though, you'll find yourself bouncing around following a particular theme, or dipping in as the mood, and the situation, dictate.

HANDBOOK A contributed volume of work on a single topic, comprising an eclectic mix of ideas, case studies, and best practices sourced by practitioners and experts in the field.

An editor or team of editors usually is appointed to seek out contributors and to evaluate content for relevance to the topic. Think of a handbook not as a ready-to-eat meal, but as a cookbook of ingredients that enables you to create the most fitting experience for the occasion.

RESOURCE Materials designed to support group learning. They come in many forms: a complete, ready-to-use exercise (such as a game); a comprehensive resource on one topic (such as conflict management) containing a variety of methods and approaches; or a collection of like-minded activities (such as icebreakers) on multiple subjects and situations.

TRAINING PACKAGE An entire, ready-to-use learning program that focuses on a particular topic or skill. All packages comprise a guide for the facilitator/trainer and a workbook for the participants. Some packages are supported with additional media—such as video—or learning aids, instruments, or other devices to help participants understand concepts or practice and develop skills.

- *Facilitator/trainer's guide* Contains an introduction to the program, advice on how to organize and facilitate the learning event, and step-by-step instructor notes. The guide also contains copies of presentation materials—handouts, presentations, and overhead designs, for example—used in the program.

- *Participant's workbook* Contains exercises and reading materials that support the learning goal and serves as a valuable reference and support guide for participants in the weeks and months that follow the learning event. Typically, each participant will require his or her own workbook.

ELECTRONIC CD-ROMs and web-based products transform static Pfeiffer content into dynamic, interactive experiences. Designed to take advantage of the searchability, automation, and ease-of-use that technology provides, our e-products bring convenience and immediate accessibility to your workspace.

METHODOLOGIES

CASE STUDY A presentation, in narrative form, of an actual event that has occurred inside an organization. Case studies are not prescriptive, nor are they used to prove a point; they are designed to develop critical analysis and decision-making skills. A case study has a specific time frame, specifies a sequence of events, is narrative in structure, and contains a plot structure—an issue (what should be/have been done?). Use case studies when the goal is to enable participants to apply previously learned theories to the circumstances in the case, decide what is pertinent, identify the real issues, decide what should have been done, and develop a plan of action.

ENERGIZER A short activity that develops readiness for the next session or learning event. Energizers are most commonly used after a break or lunch to stimulate or refocus the group. Many involve some form of physical activity, so they are a useful way to counter post-lunch lethargy. Other uses include transitioning from one topic to another, where "mental" distancing is important.

EXPERIENTIAL LEARNING ACTIVITY (ELA) A facilitator-led intervention that moves participants through the learning cycle from experience to application (also known as a Structured Experience). ELAs are carefully thought-out designs in which there is a definite learning purpose and intended outcome. Each step—everything that participants do during the activity—facilitates the accomplishment of the stated goal. Each ELA includes complete instructions for facilitating the intervention and a clear statement of goals, suggested group size and timing, materials required, an explanation of the process, and, where appropriate, possible variations to the activity. (For more detail on Experiential Learning Activities, see the Introduction to the *Reference Guide to Handbooks and Annuals*, 1999 edition, Pfeiffer, San Francisco.)

GAME A group activity that has the purpose of fostering team spirit and togetherness in addition to the achievement of a pre-stated goal. Usually contrived—undertaking a desert expedition, for example—this type of learning method offers an engaging means for participants to demonstrate and practice business and interpersonal skills. Games are effective for team building and personal development mainly because the goal is subordinate to the process—the means through which participants reach decisions, collaborate, communicate, and generate trust and understanding. Games often engage teams in "friendly" competition.

ICEBREAKER A (usually) short activity designed to help participants overcome initial anxiety in a training session and/or to acquaint the participants with one another. An icebreaker can be a fun activity or can be tied to specific topics or training goals. While a useful tool in itself, the icebreaker comes into its own in situations where tension or resistance exists within a group.

INSTRUMENT A device used to assess, appraise, evaluate, describe, classify, and summarize various aspects of human behavior. The term used to describe an instrument depends primarily on its format and purpose. These terms include survey, questionnaire, inventory, diagnostic, survey, and poll. Some uses of instruments include providing instrumental feedback to group members, studying here-and-now processes or functioning within a group, manipulating group composition, and evaluating outcomes of training and other interventions.

Instruments are popular in the training and HR field because, in general, more growth can occur if an individual is provided with a method for focusing specifically on his or her own behavior. Instruments also are used to obtain information that will serve as a basis for change and to assist in workforce planning efforts.

Paper-and-pencil tests still dominate the instrument landscape with a typical package comprising a facilitator's guide, which offers advice on administering the instrument and interpreting the collected data, and an initial set of instruments. Additional instruments are available separately. Pfeiffer, though, is investing heavily in e-instruments. Electronic instrumentation provides effortless distribution and, for larger groups particularly, offers advantages over paper-and-pencil tests in the time it takes to analyze data and provide feedback.

LECTURETTE A short talk that provides an explanation of a principle, model, or process that is pertinent to the participants' current learning needs. A lecturette is intended to establish a common language bond between the trainer and the participants by providing a mutual frame of reference. Use a lecturette as an introduction to a group activity or event, as an interjection during an event, or as a handout.

MODEL A graphic depiction of a system or process and the relationship among its elements. Models provide a frame of reference and something more tangible, and more easily remembered, than a verbal explanation. They also give participants something to "go on," enabling them to track their own progress as they experience the dynamics, processes, and relationships being depicted in the model.

ROLE PLAY A technique in which people assume a role in a situation/scenario: a customer service rep in an angry-customer exchange, for example. The way in which the role is approached is then discussed and feedback is offered. The role play is often repeated using a different approach and/or incorporating changes made based on feedback received. In other words, role playing is a spontaneous interaction involving realistic behavior under artificial (and safe) conditions.

SIMULATION A methodology for understanding the interrelationships among components of a system or process. Simulations differ from games in that they test or use a model that depicts or mirrors some aspect of reality in form, if not necessarily in content. Learning occurs by studying the effects of change on one or more factors of the model. Simulations are commonly used to test hypotheses about what happens in a system—often referred to as "what if?" analysis—or to examine best-case/worst-case scenarios.

THEORY A presentation of an idea from a conjectural perspective. Theories are useful because they encourage us to examine behavior and phenomena through a different lens.

TOPICS

The twin goals of providing effective and practical solutions for workforce training and organization development and meeting the educational needs of training and human resource professionals shape Pfeiffer's publishing program. Core topics include the following:

- Leadership & Management
- Communication & Presentation
- Coaching & Mentoring
- Training & Development
- E-Learning
- Teams & Collaboration
- OD & Strategic Planning
- Human Resources
- Consulting

What will you find on pfeiffer.com?

- The best in workplace performance solutions for training and HR professionals
- Downloadable training tools, exercises, and content
- Web-exclusive offers
- Training tips, articles, and news
- Seamless on-line ordering
- Author guidelines, information on becoming a Pfeiffer Partner, and much more

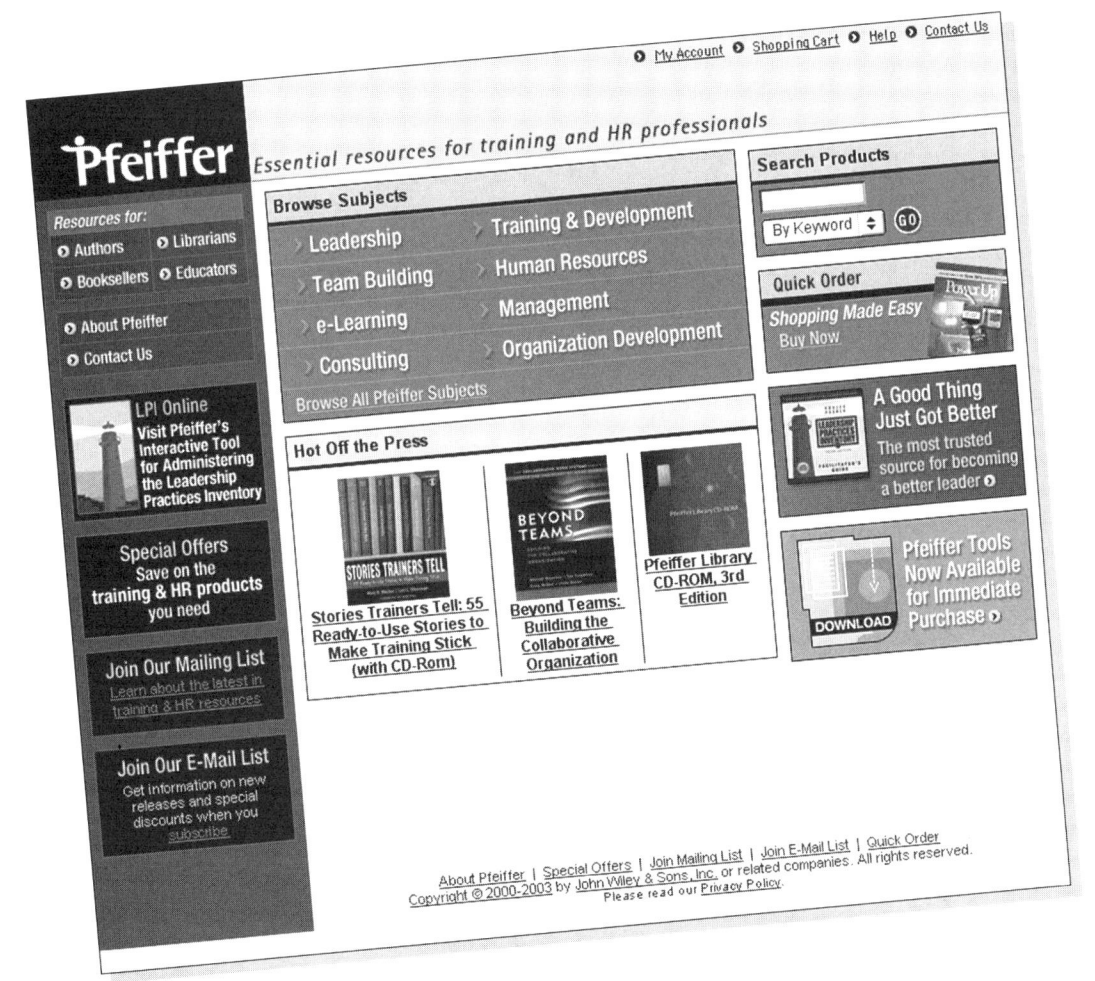

Discover more at www.pfeiffer.com

Leading Across Differences: Cases and Perspectives

Frequently Asked Questions

Edited by
Kelly M. Hannum
Belinda B. McFeeters
Lize Booysen

Pfeiffer
A Wiley Imprint
www.pfeiffer.com

Copyright © 2010 by John Wiley & Sons, Inc. All Rights Reserved.

Published by Pfeiffer
An Imprint of Wiley
989 Market Street, San Francisco, CA 94103-1741   www.pfeiffer.com

No part of this publication may be reproduced, stored in a retrieval system, or transmitted in any form or by any means, electronic, mechanical, photocopying, recording, scanning, or otherwise, except as permitted under Section 107 or 108 of the 1976 United States Copyright Act, without either the prior written permission of the Publisher, or authorization through payment of the appropriate per-copy fee to the Copyright Clearance Center, Inc., 222 Rosewood Drive, Danvers, MA 01923, 978-750-8400, fax 978-646-8600, or on the web at www.copyright.com. Requests to the Publisher for permission should be addressed to the Permissions Department, John Wiley & Sons, Inc., 111 River Street, Hoboken, NJ 07030, 201-748-6011, fax 201-748-6008, or online at http://www.wiley.com/go/permissions.

Limit of Liability/Disclaimer of Warranty: While the publisher and author have used their best efforts in preparing this book, they make no representations or warranties with respect to the accuracy or completeness of the contents of this book and specifically disclaim any implied warranties of merchantability or fitness for a particular purpose. No warranty may be created or extended by sales representatives or written sales materials. The advice and strategies contained herein may not be suitable for your situation. You should consult with a professional where appropriate. Neither the publisher nor author shall be liable for any loss of profit or any other commercial damages, including but not limited to special, incidental, consequential, or other damages.

Readers should be aware that Internet websites offered as citations and/or sources for further information may have changed or disappeared between the time this was written and when it is read.

For additional copies/bulk purchases of this book in the U.S. please contact 800-274-4434.

Pfeiffer books and products are available through most bookstores. To contact Pfeiffer directly call our Customer Care Department within the U.S. at 800-274-4434, outside the U.S. at 317-572-3985, fax 317-572-4002, or visit www.pfeiffer.com.

Pfeiffer also publishes its books in a variety of electronic formats. Some content that appears in print may not be available in electronic books.

FAQs SKU #: 978KPART10841

Facilitator's Guide Package ISBN: 9780470566893

Facilitator's Guide Set ISBN: 9780470563359

Acquiring Editors:	Lisa Shannon
Assistant Editor:	Marisa Kelley
Marketing Manager:	Tolu Babalola
Director of Development:	Kathleen Dolan Davies
Developmental Editor:	Susan Rachmeler
Production Editor:	Michael Kay
Editor:	Rebecca Taff
Manufacturing Supervisor:	Becky Morgan

Printed in the United States of America

Printing   10 9 8 7 6 5 4 3 2 1

Frequently Asked Questions

Why is this topic important?

Despite the growing challenges and opportunities created by our interconnected world, many people do not know how to lead through situations in which there are misunderstandings or conflicts rooted in differences. These types of tensions and conflicts are usually emotionally charged and very confusing. It is not clear who should take action or what, if any, action should be taken. Very little time is spent preparing leaders to understand their role and to take appropriate action. The need for practical, relevant, and usable information about how to lead across differences is growing. This package—the LAD Casebook, Facilitator's Guide, and Instructor's Guide—provides examples of and information on concepts and situations important to leading across differences. The differences addressed are steeped in social identities, such as those related to gender, religion, race, ethnicity, and country of origin.

Who is the package designed for?

The primary audience for this package is individuals with teaching or training responsibilities for new or budding managers, supervisors, or leaders who will be (or are) leading and working in groups with varied social identity groups represented. The casebook may be used in both academic and corporate settings. This package is written in a way that managers and leaders can read and reflect on the material as part of a self-study, but to reap full benefit, it is helpful to engage with others in discussions of the ideas and events shared in this package.

What is the program designed to achieve?

The package is designed to prepare leaders to lead in situations in which multiple identity groups are represented. The components provide information and tools to increase one's self-awareness about one's own perspectives and preferences, to better understand the perspectives and preferences of others, and to identify and effectively address situations wherein there is tension or conflict between identity groups in organizations.

What individual components are included in the package?

The following three components make up the *Leading Across Differences* package:

- *Leading Across Differences: Cases and Perspectives*
- *Facilitator's Guide for Leading Across Differences: Cases and Perspectives*
- *Instructor's Guide for Leading Across Differences: Cases and Perspectives*

What is included in the different components in the package?

The casebook, *Leading Across Differences: Cases and Perspectives,* is the essential component to the package. The book provides the Leadership Across Differences Framework, thirteen research-based cases, eleven chapters, nine individual exercises, and references and resources.

The Facilitator's Guide provides information on how to create and facilitate a session based on the casebook. The guide provides group debriefing suggestions as well as additional exercises intended for groups. Five chapters provide advice from practitioners about the elements of successful facilitation and session management. In addition, there are facilitation guidelines and tips.

The Instructor's Guide provides additional information specific to using the casebook in an academic setting, including sample session syllabi and five sets of PowerPoint presentations. Instructors (college professors) are invited to download these free materials from the following site:

www.wiley.com/college/hannum

If you are a trainer (and not a college professor), please send an email to the following address to receive your free copy of these materials:

pfeiffertraining@wiley.com

Which components do I need to purchase to get started?

Leading Across Differences: Cases and Perspectives provides the essential information to get started. However, we strongly recommend purchasing the Facilitator's Guide, even if you are an experienced facilitator, because facilitation of discussions about social identity differences can be more nuanced and volatile than other kinds of sessions. If you are planning an entire course or curriculum, then the Instructor's Guide provides material to help you.

How long does the program take to complete?

The package is designed to be flexible enough to use for a single one-hour session or for a semester-long course. The information in the Facilitator's Guide and Instructor's Guide will help you craft a session or series of sessions organized around specific learning outcomes.

Do I need special knowledge or skills to facilitate the program?

Facilitating sessions about social identity differences requires basic facilitation skills as well as an awareness of and sensitivity to the core issues related to differences. For this reason, we highly recommend that facilitators read the Facilitator's Guide and Instructor's Guide and complete any exercises they plan to use in a session.

What is unique about this package?

The majority of books on diversity published over the past five years have focused primarily on the role of diversity as a means to attract, develop, and retain top talent. This package uniquely addresses the challenges leaders face when building and managing diverse groups and teams.

ABOUT THE EDITORS

Kelly M. Hannum is manager of research for the EMEA Region at the Center for Creative Leadership. She holds a Ph.D. in educational research, measurement, and evaluation from the University of North Carolina at Greensboro. In addition to her work over the last fifteen years at CCL, Kelly has been involved in research and evaluation projects with organizations in a variety of sectors and countries. She is a visiting faculty member at Catholic University's IESEG School of Management in Lille, France, and teaches graduate-level courses at the University of North Carolina at Greensboro. Her work has been published and presented internationally in a variety of venues. She is the recipient of the Marcia Guttentag award from the American Evaluation Association and Young Alumni Awards from the University of North Carolina at Greensboro and Guilford College.

Belinda B. McFeeters is an independent contractor with faculty affiliations with the evaluation center at the Center for Creative Leadership, the Leadership Studies, Ph.D. Program at North Carolina A&T State University, and the Leadership Development group at the N.C. Rural Economic Development Center. She is also a freelance writer for EBSCO Publishing. Belinda earned a Ph.D. in educational leadership and policy studies from Virginia Polytechnic Institute and State University. Her primary research, evaluation, and assessment focus is on leadership development (national and global) and diversity education. Belinda has authored or co-authored several articles, book chapters, and books on higher education, multicultural education, K-12 education, cross-cultural leadership, and sociological issues.

Lize Booysen is a full professor of leadership and organizational behavior at Antioch University. Lize is an internationally recognized scholar in the field of diversity, race, gender, and leadership and a management consultant. She holds a doctorate in business leadership as well as master's degrees in clinical psychology, research psychology, and criminology, all with distinction. From 1992 until joining Antioch in 2009, Lize was full professor at the Graduate School of Business Leadership, University of South Africa. She was also the editor of the *South African Journal of Labour Relations*. Some of Lize's many awards include the GLOBE Research Award (1997) and Best Academic Achievement, University of South Africa (2004). She is also included as one of fifty role models for South African women and as leadership expert in the book *Inspirational Women @ Work* (Lapa Publishers, 2003).

ABOUT PFEIFFER'S PRODUCT LINE

Experientially based exercises and activities are a common feature of Pfeiffer's training products. Additionally, Pfeiffer offers a variety of icebreakers, energizers, team games, and simulations to energize your training and enhance the learning experience. For questions about these and other Pfeiffer products, please contact us by:

E-mail: customer@wiley.com

Phone: (U.S.) 866-888-5159; (Outside the U.S.) 317-572-3517

Mail: Customer Care Wiley/Pfeiffer, 10475 Crosspoint Blvd., Indianapolis, IN 46256

Fax: 317-572-4517

For Technical Support questions within the United States call 877-591-7762. Outside the United States call 317-572-4982.

SKU # 978KPART10841